Corporate Power and the Environment

Corporate Power and the Environment

The Political Economy of U.S. Environmental Policy

George A. Gonzalez

ROWMAN & LITTLEFIELD PUBLISHERS, INC.
Lanham · Boulder · New York · Oxford

ROWMAN & LITTLEFIELD PUBLISHERS, INC.

Published in the United States of America
by Rowman & Littlefield Publishers, Inc.
4720 Boston Way, Lanham, Maryland 20706
www.rowmanlittlefield.com

12 Hid's Copse Road, Cumnor Hill, Oxford OX2 9JJ, England

British Library Cataloging in Publication Information Available

Library of Congress Cataloging-in-Publication Data

Gonzalez, George A., 1969–
   Corporate power and the environment : the political economy of U.S. environ-
mental policy / George A. Gonzalez.
      p. cm.
   Includes bibliographical references and index.
   ISBN 0-7425-1084-0 (alk. paper)—ISBN 0-7425-1085-9 (pbk. : alk. paper)
   1. Environmental policy—United States. 2. Business and politics—United States.
I. Title.

GE180 .G66 2001
363.7'00973—dc21

                                                                00-066469

♾ ™ The paper used in this publication meets the minimum requirements of American National Standard for Information Sciences—Permanence of Paper for Printed
Library Material, ANSI/NISO Z39.48-1992.

Contents

Acknowledgments

My thoughts on state theory and environmental policy were formulated and shaped as a graduate student in the Department of Political Science at the University of Southern California. As such, I would like to thank my advisers Sheldon Kamieniecki and Howard Gillman for their advice, time, and patience. I would also like to thank Frank Janeczek for reading every word of this text, often more than once. G. William Domhoff, Jonathan West, Kenneth Shadlen, Marcus Kurtz, and Chris McMahon also deserve my gratitude and appreciation. All of them were kind and generous enough to read and comment on different portions of this manuscript. I would also like to thank the anonymous reviewers. Of course, I alone am responsible for the content and weaknesses of this book. Finally, I would like to thank the journal *Polity* for permitting me to reprint chapter 2, which initially appeared in my article, "The Conservation Policy Network, 1890–1910: The Development and Implementation of 'Practical' Forestry" (1998, vol. 31, no. 2: 269–99).

I would also like to recognize my family for their love and support. This is especially true of my mother, father, sister, paternal grandmother, and former wife, Jezabel. All of these people, in their own special way, contributed to the successful completion of this project. Finally, this book is dedicated to my cousin Sandra, who passed away at the tender age of twenty-five. Her presence and love are sorely missed.

Introduction

The arena of environmental policy is broadly viewed as an oasis of democracy in a U.S. polity often dominated by narrow and selfish special interests. When discussing the role of big business in U.S. politics, for example, scholars and laypeople alike invoke environmental policies to make the claim that the general public and science can triumph over an otherwise politically potent corporate America. In contrast to this notion, I contend throughout this book that environmental policies are largely shaped by capitalist elites and generally serve the political and economic interests of corporate America.

Just as Gabriel Kolko argued almost forty years ago in his book *The Triumph of Conservatism*, it is my position that we need to scrutinize closely the influences that shape public policies and how they operate in the U.S. political economy before we can draw any strong conclusions about who wins and loses with regard to such policies. Throughout this book I demonstrate that members of the nation's economic elite—corporate decision makers and other individuals of substantial wealth—are the dominant influences in the formation and development of U.S. environmental policies. Moreover, federal regulatory policies, such as clean air, only minimally impact on the business-as-usual operation of the U.S. economy. Additionally, federal clean air policies create a stable regulatory and political milieu for such major economic interests as automobile manufacturers and gasoline producers. Other policy areas, such as the federal government's management of the national forests and national parks, are presented to the public as a means to control economic interests and hold corporate powers in check. Instead, as I will illustrate, federal policies that manage the national forests and parks have historically altered the operation of the economy to the benefit of capitalist concerns. Furthermore, the preservation of the Redwood National Park both accommodated and served the profit goals of the large timber firms involved.

To develop a general understanding of U.S. environmental policies I focus on four environmental policy areas: management of the national forests (chap. 2), management of the national parks (chap. 3), federal wilderness preservation (chaps. 4 and 5), and federal clean air policies (chap. 6). I chose these policies because they are "hard cases" for the view that I put forward.[1] On the face of it, these cases seem unlikely to confirm the claim that economic elites are the most powerful influence in determining state behavior.

In what respect is this so? First, the management of the national forests and the national parks is carried out by well-financed and bureaucratically developed institutions—the U.S. Forest Service and National Park Service, respectively. This is in contrast to the governmental institution that manages the public grasslands and hardrock mining on the public domain—the Bureau of Land Management. This institution has historically been underdeveloped and underfinanced (Davis 1997). With the organizational structures and resources of the forest and park services at the disposal of state managers, one would expect that these managers could and would act independently of economic elites and producer groups. In the history of the national parks and the federal wilderness system, the preservation of Jackson Hole (chap. 4) and Redwood National Park (chap. 5) engendered the strongest opposition from local economic interests and timber firms (Runte 1997).

Clean air regulations on automobile and fuel emissions are relatively easy to enforce. This, for instance, is in contrast to the enforcement of hazardous waste regulations. While hundreds of rules concern the disposal of hazardous waste, thousands of sources exist for this type of waste. This makes it extremely expensive and altogether impossible to monitor all of these sources, especially with current EPA funding (Rosenbaum 1998, chap. 7; Weber 1998, chap. 3). Thus, many firms can illegally dispose of these materials with relative impunity. As a result, only 10 percent of hazardous waste is properly disposed of in the United States (Cahn 1995, 84). The sources of automobiles and gasoline, however, are comparatively few. Hence, the automobiles and fuel that violate federal clean air rules are potentially easy and relatively inexpensive to detect. Furthermore, because of the nature of these products, it is potentially simple to determine offending firms. In other words, determining the manufacturer of an automobile is simple (Bradsher 1999) compared to ascertaining the source of a hazardous chemical found in the Mississippi River or Lake Erie. Therefore, automobile manufacturers and gasoline producers would be extremely and adversely sensitive to the strengthening of regulations on automobile and fuel emissions (see Luger 2000), which did occur with the enactment of the 1990 Clean Air Act.

Therefore, given the policy outcomes and/or institutions that implement these policy regimes, one might assume that other political actors including environmental activists, elected officials, and state managers are just as important as economic elites and producer groups in the development of the policy areas of this study. I will demonstrate that they are not.

The concept of political economy that informs my argument is one that views economic systems as political systems, as cogently outlined by noted sociologists Fred Block (1990) and William Roy (1997). They describe how economic systems historically privilege certain values and interests, often at the expense of other values and interests. Capitalism—of particular relevance to this study—prioritizes profit and the interests of the capitalist class (i.e., the economic elite), often at the expense of workers and the environment.

In light of this, a central question of this study is, how have the environmental policies in question affected capitalism both as an economic and political system? Specifically, to what extent have environmental policies interjected the values of environmental protection into the operation of the economy and shielded the ecosystem from damage created by economic activity? Or have these policies largely advanced the values, economic and political interests, and preferences of economic elites and producer groups at the expense of comprehensive environmental protection and the global ecosystem?

Utilizing a political economy approach allows us to differentiate between those environmental policies that significantly alter the operation of the market and those policies that are largely symbolic. Therefore, using a political economy perspective provides a broad enough view to link conceptually the issue of who decides with the issue of whom or what benefits, why, and to what extent.

NOTE

1. Joe Feagin and his associates (1991) explain the methodological and theoretical importance of the case study approach.

Corporate Power and the Environment

1

~

The Policymaking Process

The contemporary literature on the politics of policymaking can be organized into two discrete models: plural elite/economic elite theory and the issue network/state autonomy approach.[1] In this book these competing models are evaluated using four areas of environmental policy: the management of the national forests, the management of the national parks, federal wilderness preservation, and air pollution abatement. Utilizing these policymaking models and policy areas, I am able to shed light on the relative importance of science, wealth, bureaucratic autonomy, and interest group competition in the development of public policies.

The results of this investigation will show that economic elites are the most powerful influence on public policy development and state behavior. This is because of the large amount of wealth and income that they possess and because these economic resources are readily convertible into other central resources, such as scientific expertise and public relations. Given the politically potent nature of wealth and income, those individuals who possess disproportionate amounts of these resources (i.e., economic elites) will have the greatest influence over the policymaking process. If I add the assumption that political actors are motivated by the pursuit of material and political interests, then I should also find that policy outcomes reflect the economic, political, and class interests of these wealthy actors. Environmental policies, however, are widely regarded as evidence that science and public action can triumph over corporate power and vested economic interests (e.g., Dahl 1989, 278). Nevertheless, I argue that the imperatives of capitalism, and the preferences of the dominant elites within it, overshadow science and the general public in the formation and implementation of even environmental policies.

1

Neither the plural elite/economic elite theory model nor the issue net-work/state autonomy model bodes well for the notion of a democratic American state. For the economic elite model, the public, within capitalist society, is something that is managed and kept acquiescent. Therefore, for the economic elite perspective capitalist societies are inherently undemocratic. Among the two models, the issue network/state autonomy perspective offers the greatest opportunity for democratic inputs. To the extent, however, that this approach places decision-making power in nonelected officials within the state and in scientific experts, even this view offers limited opportunities for democratic policymaking through organized interest group participation.

This chapter proceeds in the following manner. First, I will describe the development of the issue network/state autonomy model. The issue net-work/state autonomy perspective can be most aptly understood as a response to the development of the plural elite view. The plural elite perspective itself is an outgrowth of early pluralism. Second, I discuss the economic elite model. I conclude the chapter by providing an overview of the book.

ISSUE NETWORKS WITHIN PLURAL ELITISM

According to early pluralist models, the diffuse nature of political resources serves as the basis of a democratic polity and a responsive political leadership (Dahl and Lindblom 1953; Dahl 1956, 1961). The different interest groups that possess these resources use them to influence the development of specific policies. Furthermore, given regular elections, public officials must be sensitive and responsive to the citizenry in general, while interest group leaders assert direct pressure in working out the specifics of any single policy decision. Thus, according to early pluralism, as a result of political competition and elections, elected politicians are forced to bring the general interests of their constituents to the table, while interest groups bring their narrower, more specific interests and predilections into the policymaking process.

Raymond A. Bauer, Itheil De Sola Pool, and Lewis Anthony Dexter (1972) in *American Business and Public Policy* offer the following description of the policymaking process as conceptualized by pluralists. They contend that it is a process in which the positions of the various interest groups become amalgamated into one policy:

> Individual and group interests get grossly redefined by the operation of the social institutions through which they must work. The political outcome is something very different from the simple product of a parallelogram of forces input by the conflicting groups. Summing up the conflicting interests at work is only the beginning of political analysis. The heart of political analysis is the discovery of the transformation processes that make the political outputs something very different from what any of the interested parties wanted or sought. (ix)

Therefore, the policymaking process from the pluralist view is characterized as a process whereby all interested and conflicting parties' concerns, in varying degrees, are incorporated into the decision-making process and ultimately reflected in public policy. Gary Bryner (1995), for example, argues that the 1990 Clean Air Act was the result of cooperation and competition among environmental groups, industry lobbyists, and elected officials, and that these contending perspectives are reflected in the act. Roderick Nash (1982) makes similar arguments with regard to national park and wilderness preservation policies.

With the onset of racial turmoil, the Vietnam War, and Watergate during the late 1960s and early 1970s, however, criticism and skepticism of pluralism and its assumptions about power within liberal democracies quickly spread (Manley 1983; McFarland 1987; Baumgartner and Leech 1998, 88). In light of the failure of the traditional pluralist model to account for the turmoil that was besieging American political institutions and society during this period, the pluralist model underwent significant modifications. What arose from this modified version of pluralism is what Andrew McFarland (1987) terms "plural elitism" or, as John Manley (1983) refers to it, "pluralism II." The basic tenants of plural elitism contend that interest group politics in liberal democracies does not lead to a system of competing and conflicting elites but instead to a system whereby elites or specific interest groups tend to dominate those areas of government that correspond to their specific or special interests.

Plural elitism can be broken down into two distinct groups of literature. One set of plural elite literature concludes that special interest domination of specific policy areas results from skewed participation patterns and that these patterns are determined by the distribution of costs and benefits associated with participation in interest group politics. This plural elite perspective is shaped by such theorists as Murray Edelman (1964, 1971, 1988), Mancur Olson (1971), and Theodore Lowi (1979). The second set of plural elite authors contends that the central factor that creates special interest dominance is the distribution of power in liberal capitalist societies. This second plural elite view is reflected in Dahl and Lindblom (1976), Lindblom (1977), and, to a lesser extent, McConnell (1966).

Lowi (1979) argues that the inability of the president and Congress to properly regulate special interests has led to deeply flawed public policies, as well as to the vitiating of democratic energies. He contend that due to the legislative practices of the post–World War II period, at both the executive and congressional levels, special interests have been able to "capture" federal agencies (subgovernments). These legislative practices allow agencies to set policies in critical areas. This delegation on the part of the Congress and the president is predicated on the belief that pluralism is the actual process that is taking place at the agency level. This assumption, which Lowi contends is dominant within both government and academia, is called "interest group liberalism."

Hence, as a result of the philosophy of interest group liberalism, wide discretion is afforded governmental agencies to set policies, because it is assumed that policy decisions will be worked out by federal agencies and competing interest groups. Lowi argues that by delegating important policy questions from the president and the Congress to federal agencies, legislators are in effect preventing the development of effective public policies and substantive pluralist politics. With the absence of legislative guidance, agencies most readily rely on the policy preferences of those groups most affected by the particular agency. In describing Medicaid policy, Lowi (1979) finds the same ailments that afflict all those policy areas permeated by interest group liberalism: "It [Medicaid policy] is that same political process we have noted all through the analysis of interest-group liberalism—the decline of a public awareness, the decline of democratic conflict, the reduction of government to the preferences of the agencies and the clientele most concerned with a particular program" (232).

Explicit in Lowi's critique of interest group liberalism is the failure of groups representing the public interest to materialize and represent the general good. Both Edelman (1964, 1971, 1988) and Olson (1971) offer explanations to account for the relative lack of political mobilization among the general populace and, in turn, for why narrow special interests are mobilized and thus able to dominate specific policy areas. Olson offers a traditional economic cost–benefit analysis to explain the state of interest group politics as described by Lowi. Olson contends special interest dominance is rooted in the distribution of costs and benefits associated with participation in the interest group process. He argues that the general populace remains largely immobilized and unorganized, because from the individual's perspective, it does not make economic sense to mobilize and to contribute to an organization whose sole purpose is to represent politically the common good. This is because among large groups it is unclear from an individual perspective whether his or her contribution to a mobilization or organizational effort will make a significant impact. Furthermore, any gains made on behalf of the common good by an organization will be shared by everyone regardless of whether any particular person helped in achieving the gains.

In contrast, among smaller groups, such as business trade associations, the apparent distribution of costs and benefits encourages mobilization and organization. In small groups it is more readily apparent to the individual member the impact that his or her contribution will make toward achieving a group goal. Within small groups it is also more apparent to the individual member what benefits he or she will receive for his or her contribution associated with achieving group goals. Second, it is also more readily apparent to other group members when a particular member does not make his or her allotted contribution. In light of this transparency, the withholding of a contribution by one member will jeopardize the group objective, because members will be less willing to contribute if other members withhold their contribution. The mobilization and organization of successful special interests with large memberships, such as farmers and the medical profession, are not predicated on the gains made by the achievement of political goals. Instead, successful organization among special interests with broad membership is motivated by nonpolitical benefits associated with membership within professional and occupational organizations—benefits such as technical knowledge distributed exclusively to members and insurance coverage offered exclusively to members.

Edelman (1964, 1971, 1988) also applies a cost–benefit analysis to account for the lack of mobilization among the populace and for the dominance of narrow special interests. Unlike Olson, however, Edelman does not couch his cost–benefit assessment in terms of economics. Instead, he argues that the ability of special interests to dominate specific policy areas is associated with the benefits received from symbols. Edelman holds that the general public is placated by the psychological and social benefits associated with the symbols generated by public policy and political rhetoric, whereas more narrowly construed interest groups, or special interests, tend to be only satisfied with economic or instrumental benefits. Hence, given the pattern of demands outlined by Edelman, the general public is provided with low-cost symbols, while special interests are provided with the tangible benefits doled out by public policies.

Drawing heavily on Edelman's work, Matthew Cahn (1995) avers that post-1970 environmental regulatory policies (i.e., clean air, clean water, energy, and waste policies) can be most aptly characterized as symbolic responses to the public's growing environmental concerns, rather than as substantive efforts to regulate corporate America. He arrives at this conclusion by analyzing the content of these policies, which Cahn juxtaposes against the federal government's continued encouragement of economic growth and continued support and subsidization of fossil fuels usage (e.g., the Persian Gulf War). These are the primary factors that cause air and water pollution, as well as waste creation (also see Christoff 1996). The federal government's subsidizing and encouragement of fossil fuel usage is reflected in its 1998 appropriation of $200 billion for the maintenance and expansion of the nation's transportation infrastructure, which "amounted to the largest public-works program in the nation's history" (Andrews 1999, 303). Over 80 percent of these funds were dedicated to highway and bridge construction (Andrews 1999, 303–4).

Despite the barriers described by Edelman and Olson to the creation of public interest lobbies, the 1960s and the early 1970s did see the expansion of the number of public interest organizations, and the activation of public interest advocates (Walker 1983; 1991, chap. 4; Baumgartner and Leech 1998, 103). During this period, environmental groups, in particular, increased significantly in number, membership, and staff (Baumgartner and Jones 1993, 187; Lowry 1998, 47; Shaiko 1999; Rose 2000). These newly created groups, and advocates, have been participating in such issue and policy areas as the environment, health care, consumer affairs, race relations, good government, and poverty (for examples, see Heinz et al. 1993). It is these public interest advocates and groups that Hugh Heclo (1978) views as the primary challenge to the relationship between special interests and subgovernments as described by Lowi. With the introduction of these actors, the relationship between government agencies and interest groups has been transformed from capture to one of issue networks. Heclo (1978) argues:

> It would be foolish to suggest that the clouds of issue networks that have accompanied expanding national policies are set to replace the more familiar politics of subgovernments in Washington. What they are doing is to overlay the once stable political reference points with new forces that complicate calculations, decrease predictability, and impose considerable strains on those charged with government leadership. The overlay of networks and issue politics not only confronts but also seeps down into the formerly well-established politics of particular policies and programs. (105)

Therefore, with the expansion of federal programs into new areas, such as air pollution, medical care for the poor, urban renewal, and civil rights, public interest organizations and individuals have entered into the policy fray, thus challenging the near monopoly on information, perspective, and other political resources held by heretofore unchallenged special interests.

It is important, however, to note that public interest groups and advocates were active in certain public policy areas prior to the 1960s. Significant for our discussion is the fact that since the late nineteenth century, nonbusiness groups and individuals have been active on the issue of federal land management. There is no denying, however, that these groups, individuals, and perspectives substantially multiplied during the 1960s and early 1970s.

Heclo points to energy policy during the Carter administration as an example of what he feels is the result of expanding and increasingly complex issue networks.

> The debate on energy policy is rich in examples of the kaleidoscopic interaction of changing issue networks. The Carter administration's initial proposal was worked out among experts who were closely tied in to conservation-minded networks. Soon it became clear that those concerned with macroeconomic policies had been largely bypassed in the planning, and last-minute amendments were made in the proposal presented to Congress, a fact that was not lost on the networks of leading economists and economic correspondents. Once congressional consideration began, it quickly became evident that attempts to define the energy debate in terms of a classic confrontation between big oil companies and consumer interest were doomed. More and more policy watchers joined in the debate, bringing to it their own concerns and analyses: tax reformers, nuclear

power specialists, civil rights groups interested in more jobs; the list soon grew beyond the wildest dreams of the original energy policy planners. (1978, 104)

Therefore, these issue networks have in a significant sense remedied the classic Schnattschneider (1960) dilemma. Namely, issue networks have, according to Heclo and others (e.g., Bosso 1987; Baumgartner and Jones 1993; Browne 1995; Baumgartner and Leech 1998, 111–14; McCool 1998; Sabatier 1999), successfully expanded the "scope of conflict." Now broader public interests are generally incorporated into policy deliberations.

Heclo's prognosis of subgovernment relations, however, runs into difficulty when one considers the second variant of plural elite arguments. This second group of plural elite authors hold that the existence of public interest advocates to challenge entrenched special interests with data, a new perspective, and public attention is going to have little impact. This is because for this set of authors the ability of special interests to capture segments of the state does not rest on the fact that government/special interest relations have historically been unmonitored and unchallenged but on the power of special interests themselves.[2] For this perspective within plural elitism, it is the resources controlled by special interests, especially business interests, that allow them to capture significant segments of the state. This could help explain why, despite the increasing challenge raised by growing environmental groups, producer groups continue to exercise dominant influence over those public policies that manage hardrock mining and livestock grazing on the public lands (Wilkinson 1992, chaps. 2 and 3; Klyza 1994, 1996; Davis 1997).

Grant McConnell (1966), like Lowi, attributes the diffusion of state power to a dominant political philosophy. This political philosophy, according to McConnell, is rooted in discourses developed during the Progressive era. These discourses posit that democracy is most effectively applied in small bureaucratic units. In turn, this fracturing of the federal government into a multitude of small units allows the capture of significant amounts of state power by special interests. Hence, while both McConnell and Lowi trace the public philosophy that has predicated the creation of a governmental structure that promotes capture by special interests to different philosophical precepts, both their conclusions are similar.

Although McConnell, however, does not make it a central part of his thesis, he does make references throughout his book to the power of those special interests that are able to capture portions of governmental policy. At one point he writes:

One consequence [of the diffusion of the governmental structure] . . . is to expose government to the play of favoritism and arbitrariness, and to make politics the preserve of those who are already economically or socially powerful. It is to surrender the peculiar functions of government to private hands over which many who must feel government power can have no influence. Self-government in this sense may enlarge the freedom of the powerful, but it may also diminish the freedom of the weak. (1966, 194)

Thus, unlike Lowi, who seems to suggest that all that is necessary for a special interest to capture a segment of state power is organization and a heightened interest in a particular state function, McConnell does tie the ability to capture a segment of state policy to the power of the specific interest group. Therefore, he introduces the differing levels of power that special interests possess as a variable in special interest politics.

In light of this variable, McConnell (1966) points to the relative political weakness of labor unions to explain its lack of a powerful governmental ally:

Labor unions were not only weak politically; they had no desire to become strong. By the 1930s the Department of Labor was subject to Washington jibes as "the Department of Labor Statistics"—a cutting characterization in a power-oriented city which assumed that the significance of any group could be measured by the weight of the part of government it owned. (303)

Labor's relative weakness in the special interest process is in sharp contrast to that of business, as shown by McConnell's case studies. According to McConnell, business interests, at both the federal and local levels were able to exercise firm control over significant aspects of governmental policy.[3] A certain parallel can be observed between McConnell's description of the Department of Labor and the historic behavior of the Environmental Protection Agency (EPA). Despite its broad legislative authority and the support of the environmental community, the EPA has failed to develop an aggressive regulatory regime—one that would significantly and substantially modify the behavior of corporate America (Yeager 1991; Cahn 1995; Mintz 1995; Cushman 1998; Weber 1998).

While Lowi tends to ignore the power of business relative to other groups, and McConnell implies its superiority, Robert Dahl and Charles Lindblom (1976) assert business's superior power position as part of a significant modification to their earlier elaborations of the pluralist model. According to these authors, business's superior power is derived from the fact that corporations are charged by society to organize and manage its productive forces. The result of this responsibility is the "privileged participation of business" in government:

Businessmen are not ordered by law to perform the many organizational and leadership tasks that are delegated to them. All these societies operate by rules that require that businessmen be induced rather than commanded. It is therefore clear that these societies must provide sufficient benefits or indulgences to businessmen to constitute an inducement for them to perform their assigned tasks.

The consequence of these arrangements—peculiar as they would appear to a man from Mars—is that it becomes a major task of government to design and maintain an inducement system for businessmen, to be solicitous of business interests, and to grant to them, for its value as an incentive, an intimacy of participation in government itself. In all these respects the relation between government and business is unlike the relation between government and any other group in the society. (Dahl and Lindblom 1976, xxxvii)

Hence, for the plural elitists, political resources are no longer limited to those resources directly associated with elections—such as votes, money, and prestige—but now are expanded to include the authoritative power that business leaders exercise over a society's economy. In turn, this authoritative control is proffered to explain the dominance that business groups exercise in the policymaking process. Indeed, this acknowledgment can help explain why certain agencies that benefited racial minorities and the poor lost funding or were altogether eliminated during the 1980s (Piven and Cloward 1982), while those agencies that serviced business interests went relatively undisturbed.

In addition to the power that Dahl and Lindblom ascribe to business based on its control of society's productive forces, Lindblom (1977) also argues that business can exercise dominant influence over those areas of governmental policy over which it does not have a priori dominance. He argues that it can exercise this influence because of the substantial and disproportionate amount of resources under the direction of businesspeople and corporate leaders:

No other group of citizens can compare with businessmen, even roughly, in effectiveness in the polyarchal [pluralist] process. How so? Because, unlike any other group of citizens, they can draw on the resources they command as public "officials" [leaders of corporations] to support their activities in polyarchal politics. (194)

Kay Schlozman and John Tierney's (1986) comprehensive study of interest groups, for example, documents the substantial advantage in resources, particularly money, that corporate and trade lobbies have over most public interest lobbies. Additionally, their study also suggests the importance of money in the policymaking process (also see West and Loomis 1999).

As a result of the political power that he attributes to business elites, Lindblom, in a response to an article written by Manley (1983), declares himself to be a ".4" pluralist:

Roughly speaking, I have suggested, politics is pluralist only on secondary issues, not on primary issues.

If, for that reason alone, I could count myself only a .5 pluralist, I must reduce my commitment to pluralist theory again—say, down to about .4—to acknowledge that among the secondary day-to-day issues that reach the political agenda are many to which public attention is not attracted and which are settled largely by interchange greatly restricted to businessmen and government officials. (384–85)

Given this view of the policymaking process, it would appear that increased political activity and competition around issue areas are only going to have a marginal impact on the development of U.S. public policies.

ISSUE NETWORKS WITHIN STATE AUTONOMY THEORY

The second perspective within plural elitism is taken into account by the theoretical approach developed by Stephen Krasner (1978), Theda Skocpol (1979, 1985), Eric Nordlinger (1981), and Stephen Skowronek (1982). This approach has been termed *state autonomy theory*. At the core of state autonomy theory is the notion that the state is able to behave independently of all societal groups. This idea is cogently expressed by Skocpol (1992) in the following:

> Because states are authoritative and resourceful organizations—collectors of revenue, centers of cultural authority, and hoarders of means of coercion—they are sites of autonomous action, not reducible to the demands or preferences of any social group. Both appointed and elected officials have ideas and organizational and career interests of their own, and they devise and work for policies that will further those ideas and interests, or at least not harm them. (44)

Therefore, because states are invested with responsibilities, resources, and authority, elected politicians and appointed officials—who control the state's resources and authority—can and do behave independently of social groups. This includes business interests (Skocpol 1980, 160–69; 1992, 26–30 and 53–54).

Skocpol, for one, contends that officials within the state operate freely within a restricted policy area in formulating policy. Within this space, "autonomous" officials cannot only contribute significantly to policy formulation, but they can help mobilize constituencies, expand existing programs, develop state capacities, and take preemptive action (Skocpol 1985). Given the space within which officials operate, the beliefs, ideologies, and training of elected politicians and appointed officials become important explanatory variables in analyzing public policies. Christopher Klyza (1992), for example, explains that the U.S. Forest Service during the Progressive era was a growing and bureaucratically developed agency. He argues this state structure facilitated the autonomous behavior of officials within the service. These officials were guided by professional forestry.

According to state autonomy theorists, several factors contribute to public officials' ability to behave autonomously, including the professionalization of the bureaucracy, the development of state capabilities, and the existence of well-developed issue networks from which state officials can draw policy ideas and plans. Skowronek (1982, chaps. 3 and 6), for example, outlines the development of civil service laws, and the subsequent professionalization of the federal bureaucracy, during the Progressive era to argue how this professionalization enhanced the capacity of the state and increased its autonomy. Similarly, the Department of Agriculture, according to Skocpol and Kenneth Finegold, played an influential role in formulating the Agriculture Adjustment Act of 1933. It was able to incorporate an approach toward agriculture price stabilization that was not advocated by the farm lobby. The department was able to do so because it had a professional and well-developed information gathering and policy formulation infrastructure already in place when the move toward price stabilization started (Skocpol and Finegold 1982, 268–75; Finegold and Skocpol 1995).

Both James Q. Wilson (1980) and McFarland (1987, 1991, 1992), while not donning the rubric of state autonomy, have developed models of policymaking that emphasize the ability of state actors to act independently of powerful business interests.[4] Wilson contends that, as a result of interest group interaction and electoral competition, state officials can behave independently of powerful business groups and impose costly regulations on these groups. Indicative of Wilson's model, Charles O. Jones (1975) contends that the content of the 1970 Clean Air Act was determined by the anticipated electoral competition expected to take place between Senator Edward Muskie and President Richard Nixon in the 1972 presidential election. This anticipated competition led to what Jones called *speculative augmentation*, whereby Muskie and Nixon outdid each other in developing the 1970 Clean Air Act to attract the growing environmental vote. As a result of this, the act bestows substantial regulatory powers on the federal government.

McFarland (1987), for one, views Wilson's theoretical perspective as a promising approach in the reenergizing of pluralist thought that had been otherwise enervated by the events of the late 1960s and early 1970s. He (1991, 1992) offers additional circumstances under which state officials can behave autonomously to counter the preferences and interests of business groups. McFarland (1991), for instance, argues that American politics can be analyzed according to reform cycles. Under these cycles, society at large periodically demands reform of business behavior. These periodic popular demands for reform allow and prompt state leaders to act autonomously against the interests of business. The 1900s, 1930s, and 1960s are the decades during which these reform periods took place. McFarland (1992) adds that issue networks, interest group patrons (Walker 1983, 1991), and social movements (Tarrow 1994) can all serve as factors that contribute to autonomous behavior on the part of the state. The environmental legislation of the early 1970s can be seen as an outgrowth of the 1960s reform period, as well as a result of the growing pro-environment social movement. In addition, Jeffrey Berry (1977, 72–74) explains that some environmental groups in the 1970s were substantially aided by interest group patrons, both public and private (also see Dowie 1995, 35–38).

It has been Skocpol, among state autonomy theorists, who has most directly incorporated issue networks in her analysis of public policy. When state actors, according to Skocpol, glean ideas and whole policy plans from such organizations as the Brookings Institute, the Heritage Foundation, or the Rand Corporation, they are acting autonomously because the plans developed within these organizations are developed by experts that she believes take a class-neutral approach to policy questions. She contends with respect to such experts that "most often . . . they [experts from issue networks] attempt to act as 'third-force' mediators, downplaying the role of class interests and class struggles and promoting the expansion of state or other 'public' capacities to regulate the economy and social relations" (1986/87, 332). Hence, for Skocpol, because many of the plans developed within issue networks are not reflective of any one group's perspective, the incorporation of these plans into public policy represent instances of autonomous behavior on the part of public officials. State officials adopt these plans because they offer a rational and scientific means of regulating societal and economic relations. Samuel Hays's (1959) work on conservation policies during the Progressive era is consistent with Skocpol's approach. He argues that autonomous officials within the federal government incorporated scientific discourses into these policies.

The relationship between issue networks and state actors proffered by Skocpol is consistent with the view that Heclo has of issue network/government relations. Within the milieu of ever-complex and competitive issue networks described by Heclo, public officials are able to draw together their governing coalition from a wide spectrum of choices. In other words, with the proliferation of public interest groups as well as other policy activists, elected and appointed officials can draw their agendas and positions from a variety of individuals, groups and thus perspectives. Heclo (1978) argues:

> The proliferation of . . . networks of policy watchers offers new strategic resources for public managers. These are mainly opportunities to split and recombine the many sources of support and opposition that exist on policy issues. Of course, there are limits on how far a political executive can go in shopping for a constituency, but the general tendency over time has been to extend those limits. (117)

Therefore, the existence of competing policy activists and groups have increased the possibilities for state officials to draw on groups and individuals outside of entrenched special interests in determining the shape and content of policies.

Issue networks play a prominent role in Skocpol's analysis of the public policies directed toward mothers and children during the post–World War I period (1992; Skocpol et al. 2000). In fact, issue networks were so important in developing these policies that Skocpol significantly modifies her theoretical approach when analyzing them. Instead of utilizing a state-centered approach in analyzing welfare policies during the Progressive era and post–World War I period, Skocpol uses what she terms a *polity-centered approach*. By using the more expansive phrase of "polity" as opposed to "state," Skocpol is including in her analysis issue networks and party structures, both of which she deems as central to understanding welfare policies during this period. In the case of welfare policies dealing with mothers' and children's issues, Skocpol argues that it was a national network of women activists and women's clubs that provided public officials both the policy ideas and the political energy for the development of such policies. Similarly, Michael Kraft (1994) argues that it was the intersection of positively disposed political leaders, public opinion, environmental groups, and scientific studies that lead to the formulation and enactment of the 1990 Clean Air Act.

With the creation of the polity-centered (or state autonomy/issue networks) perspective, in many respects we have come back to the early pluralist model (Domhoff 1996, chap. 8). Both models emphasize the role of public officials and competing interest groups in the development of public policy (Almond 1988). The significant difference between pluralism and state autonomy/issue networks is the role of business. Under early pluralism, business was only one interest group among many. The polity-centered perspective, in contrast, acknowledges that business and industry are the most powerful interest groups in American politics and that usually their will can only be thwarted under specific and narrow circumstances. Nevertheless, while these defeats are normally limited in scope, they can be costly, both politically and monetarily. Environmental policies, both pre- and post-1970, are viewed as some of the most significant defeats of corporate America in U.S. history (Nash 1982; Schrepfer 1983; Bosso 1987; Klyza 1992, 1996; Bryner 1995; Kraft 1994, 1997; Rosenbaum 1998; Weber 1998).

ECONOMIC ELITE THEORY

Elite theorists, in contrast to pluralists, have historically argued that power in the United States, and other advanced nations, is highly concentrated (Mills 1956; Dye 1990; Hayward 1998; Parsons 1999). One set of elite theorists argues that political power is especially concentrated in the highest echelons of the corporate community and among individuals of substantial wealth (Weinstein 1968; Miliband 1969; Eakins 1969; 1972; Kolko 1977; Domhoff 1978, 1998; Barrow 1993, chap. 1). I refer to this variant of elite theory as *economic elite theory*. While plural elite theorists describe how individual corporate decision makers dominate specific and narrow policy areas, economic elite theorists contend that these corporate decision makers, along with other individuals of wealth, develop and impose broadly construed policies on the state. Additionally, while the plural elite perspective views the business community as socially and politically fragmented, proponents of the economic elite model

hold that the owners and leadership of this community can be most aptly characterized as composing a coherent social and political unit or class.

Clyde Barrow (1993) points out that "typically, members of the capitalist
class [or the economic elite] are identified as those persons who manage corporations and/or own those corporations." He adds that this group composes
no more than 0.5 to 1.0 percent of the total U.S. population (17). This group
as a whole is the upper class and the upper echelon of the corporate or business community. The resource that members of the economic elite possess
that allow them to exercise a high level of influence over the state is wealth.
The wealth and income of the economic elite allow it to accumulate superior
amounts of other valuable resources, such as social status, deference, prestige,
organization, campaign finance, lobbying, political access, and legal and scientific expertise (Barrow 1993, 16).

According to the economic elite perspective, despite the segmentation of
the economic elite along lines that are related to their material holdings, most
policy differences that arise due to differences in economic interests can be and
are mediated. There are social and organizational mechanisms that exist that
allow business leaders to resolve difficulties that may develop within a particular segment and between different segments of the corporate community.
For specific industries, or for disagreements between different industries,
trade or business associations can serve as organizations to mediate corporate
conflict. Social institutions, such as social and country clubs, can also serve as
means through which to develop political consensus among the upper echelon of the business community on various economic, political, and social issues
(Domhoff 1974). Michael Useem (1984), based on his extensive study of large
American and British corporations, argues that corporate directors who hold
membership on more than one board of directors tend to serve as a means
through which the corporate community achieves consensus on various political issues (also see Mintz and Schwartz 1985).

For broad issues, business leaders are also able to arrive at policy agreement
and consensus through "policy-planning networks." According to G. William
Domhoff, the policy-planning network is composed of four major components:
policy discussion groups, foundations, think tanks, and university research institutes. This network's budget, in large part, is drawn directly from the corporate
community. Furthermore, many of the directors and trustees of the organizations that comprise this policy-planning network are often drawn directly from
the upper echelons of the corporate community and from the upper class. These
trustees and directors, in turn, help set the general direction of the policy-
planning organizations, as well as directly choose the individuals that manage
the day-to-day operation of these organizations (Domhoff 1998, chap. 4). Many
environmental groups, in terms of their leadership and/or financing, have the
characteristics of economic elite–led policy-planning organizations. These
groups include the Sierra Club prior to the 1960s, the Save-the-Redwood

League, and the Environmental Defense Fund (Jones 1965; Schrepfer 1983; Cohen 1988; Snow 1992; Dowie 1995). The Environmental Defense Fund, for example, has several corporate executives on its board of directors (Dowie 1995, 58–59).

Domhoff (1978) describes the political behavior of those members of the economic elite that manage and operate within the policy-planning network:

> The policy-formation process is the means by which the power elite formulates policy on larger issues. It is within the organizations of the policy-planning network that the various special interests join together to forge, however, slowly and gropingly, the general policies that will benefit them as a whole. It is within the policy process that the various sectors of the business community transcend their interest-group consciousness and develop an overall class consciousness. (61)

Therefore, according to the economic elite model, those members of the economic elite that operate within the policy-planning network take on a broad perspective and act on behalf of the economic elite as a whole. Within this policy-planning network, members of the economic elite take general positions on such issues as foreign policy, economic policy, business regulation, and defense policy questions (Weinstein 1968; Eakins 1969, 1972; Kolko 1977; Domhoff 1978, chap. 4; 1998, chap. 4; Barrow 1993, chap. 1).

This broad perspective also allows the policy-planning network to develop plans and positions to deal with other groups and classes. Thus, the network develops positions and plans concerning such policy areas as welfare, environmental, and education policies. These plans can take several forms depending on the scope and level of the problems facing the business community and the state (Weinstein 1968; Eakins 1972; Domhoff 1978, 1990, 1996, 1998; Barrow 1990; 1993, chap. 1).

Domhoff argues that the focal point in the policy-planning network is the policy discussion group. The other components of the policy-planning network—foundations, think tanks, and university research institutes—generally provide original research, policy specialists, and ideas to the policy discussion groups (Domhoff 1978, 63). Policy discussion groups are largely composed of members from the corporate community and the upper class. Examples of such groups are the Council on Foreign Relations, the Committee for Economic Development, the National Association of Manufacturers, and the Chamber of Commerce. Overall, policy discussion groups are the arenas where members of the economic elite come together with policy specialists to formulate policy positions and where members of the economic elite evaluate policy specialists for possible service in government (Eakins 1972; Domhoff 1978, 61–87; 1998, chap. 4; Barrow 1993, chap. 1).[5] One example of a policy discussion group is the American Forestry Association. It is a timber industry discussion group established during the late nineteenth century to deal with issues regarding forest management (see chap. 2 of this book). In the 1980s, the corporate community organized the Clean Air Working Group, a policy discussion group focused on the issue of federal clean air regulations (see chap. 6 of this book).

THE POLICY-PLANNING NETWORK AND THE STATE

According to the economic elite model, the corporate dominated policy-planning network has several points of access to the policymaking process within the state. Members of the economic elite will often directly lobby Congress and the executive bureaucracy on behalf of ideas developed within the network. As I describe in chapters 3, 4, and 5, economic elite lobbying efforts have had a significant impact on the development of the National Park Service and wilderness preservation policies. Participation of the policy-planning network in the policymaking process also takes place in a direct and formal manner. The policy network and the corporate community directly influence the policymaking process through the Business Council, the Business Round-table, and appointments to government (Domhoff 1998, chap. 7).

The Business Council was created in 1933 as a quasi-governmental advisory group. Its members are mostly the chairpersons or presidents of the largest corporations. Also, many members of the council are also members of other policy groups, such as the Committee for Economic Development or the Council on Foreign Relations. Despite the fact that it became independent in 1962, the Business Council still holds its regular consultative meetings with government officials. During these three-day meetings, council members interact with government officials through formally planned political functions, such as policy speeches and panels, and through the recreational activities that are held throughout the three-day session. The expenses for the entire session are paid by corporate leaders. Domhoff (1978) argues:

> The Business Council is centrally situated in the policy-planning network. It is a collecting and consensus-seeking point for much of the work of the other organizations. Moreover, it is one of the few organizations that has regular and formal meetings with government officials. It is, then, a major connection between big business and government. In a way, its centrality among the policy groups makes it the unofficial board of directors within the power elite. (72)

While the Business Council is viewed as a consultative body that meets with government officials in an informal setting, its lobbying counterpart is the Business Roundtable. The roundtable is a lobbying group composed of the chief executive officers (CEOs) of the two hundred largest U.S. companies. Many members of the roundtable are also members of the Business Council (Domhoff 1998, 156–59). Its members directly lobby Congress, as well as have private meetings with the president and cabinet members. Domhoff (1978) points out, "The Business Council prefers to remain in the background and focus on the Executive Branch, the Business Roundtable is unique among general policy groups in that it has an activist profile and personally lobbies members of Congress as readily as it meets privately with the President and cabinet leaders" (79). The issues on which the Business Roundtable lobbies the government are usually of a general nature and not tied to any one industry. It, for example, lobbied strongly against a proposed version of the 1990 Clean Air Act that was viewed as unacceptable by several sectors of the corporate community (chap. 6 of this book).

The most direct means that the corporate community and policy-planning network have of impacting the policymaking process is through the governmental appointment process. Ralph Miliband (1969, chap. 5)argues that the governmental appointment process in advanced capitalist countries leads to the appointment of individuals who are disposed to the capitalist status quo and to businesspeople's policy predilections. A relevant example of this would be that of the Environmental Protection Agency (EPA) director during the first Bush administration, William Reilly. Before becoming EPA director, Reilly was director of both the Environmental Defense Fund and the Conservation Fund. Both of these organizations are leaders in what Mark Dowie (1995, chap. 5) calls *third wave environmentalism*. He views the advocates and adherents of this movement as conservative environmentalists because key in their thinking "is the notion that production decisions should remain in the private sector and that removing market barriers and government subsidies that promote environmentally unsound practices will allow the mechanisms of the marketplace to motivate industries to make environmental protection profitable" (108). Dowie goes on to argue that "another implicit tenet of the third-wave ideology is that all non-fraudulent businesses and industries deserve to exist, even if their technologies or products are irreversibly degrading to the environment" (108).

On a broader level, Philip Burch, Jr.'s (1980/81), extensive study of cabinet, subcabinet, diplomatic, and Supreme Court appointments demonstrates how a strong majority of government appointees throughout American history have been drawn from the upper echelons of the corporate community or the upper class or had strong ties to either one or both of these groups.[6] Therefore, members of the economic elite have historically relied on appointments to government to have superior access to the policy formulation and implementation process (Mintz 1975).

After reviewing the backgrounds of those individuals appointed to cabinet level, subcabinet, and presidential advisory positions (Domhoff 1987; 1998, 247–56), Domhoff (1998) concludes:

The general picture that emerges from this information on the overrepresentation of members of the corporate community in appointed governmental positions is that the highest levels of the executive branch, especially in the State, Defense, and Treasury departments, are interlocked constantly with the corporate community through the movement of executives and lawyers in and out of government. . . . This system gives corporate officials temporary independence from the narrow concerns of their own companies and allows them to perform the more general roles they have learned in the policy-discussion groups. (253, 255)

Therefore, through this intimate and constant relationship among the corporate community, the policy network, and the executive branch, the policy proposals formulated in the policy-planning network are directly injected into the governmental policymaking process. Two members of the economic elite, for example—Gifford Pinchot and Stephen Mather—were appointed to director positions within the U.S. Forest Service and the National Park Service at the time of these agencies' inceptions. They were also leading members of policy-planning networks. As a result of Pinchot's and Mather's appointments, ideas developed within their respective networks were incorporated into the public policies of both the forest and park services (chaps. 2 and 3 of this book).

OVERVIEW OF THE BOOK

The four policy areas examined in this book are ideal arenas to appraise competing policymaking models. (Table 1.1 describes some of the key points of convergence and diverge among these competing models.) One key reason for this is that environmental policies are widely perceived to be arenas where business influence is weakest (e.g., Dahl 1989, 278). These specific environmental policy areas, furthermore, hold additional theoretical and historical significance. First, these policies all developed within the milieu of complex and competing issue networks. Thus, by examining these policy areas, I can evaluate the validity of the state autonomy/issue network perspective. Second, an analysis of the development of these policies can help us determine whether Heclo or Domhoff's description of these networks is most accurate. In other words, are issue/policy networks fragmented as Heclo suggests, or do economic elites coordinate, manage, and integrate significant portions of these networks as Domhoff posits?

A second theoretical issue of this study relates to the development of state institutions and professionalism. Specifically, the professionalism that inheres in the U.S. Forest Service and the National Park Service (Kunioka and Rothenberg 1993; Lowry 1994), and their bureaucratic expansion, make them ideal candidates for the type of autonomous behavior predicted by the state autonomy perspective. In addition, the U.S. Forest Service has historically been among the most successful of state agencies in incorporating professionalism and efficient administrative techniques within its bureaucratic

Table 1.1   **Competing Policymaking Models**

Policy Formulation Models	Loci of Political Power	Business Political Behavior*	Description of Policy Formulation Process	Policy Outcomes
Pluralism	Numerous interest groups and elected officials	Fragmented	Interest groups, rooted in different segments of society, competing vigorously	Shaped by competing interest groups and elected officials
Plural elite	Various interest groups	Coordinated to limited extent through trade associations	Different interest groups, especially business groups, dominating different policy areas	Special interests determine the content of narrowly construed policies
State autonomy/ issue networks	State officials supported by issue networks	Fragmented	State officials draw ideas, plans, and support from issue networks to develop policies	Appointed and elected officials determine the content of policies
Economic elite	Individuals of wealth and corporate decision makers	Largely coordinated through policy-planning networks and other social and business institutions	Economic elites, operating through policy-planning networks, dominate the policy formulation process	The policy preferences of economic elites pre-dominate

*Refers to *Fortune 800* firms.

structure (Kaufman 1960; Klyza 1992, 1994, 1996; Clarke and McCool 1996). Therefore, in chapters 2 and 3, the focus of my analysis of both the forest and park services will be the development of these organizations' professional precepts and the implications that these precepts have had for public policy formulation and implementation. This requires that I examine the historic and political circumstances within which these precepts developed, which was during the Progressive era.

After discussing the forest and park services, I next turn our attention to the development of wilderness preservation policy (chaps. 4 and 5). I specifically examine the incorporation of three wilderness areas into the national park system: Yosemite, Jackson Hole, and Redwood National Park. The incorporation of these areas into the national park system will provide us with significant insight into the historic operation of the U.S. wilderness preservation issue/policy network. Apart from shedding light on the operation of issue/policy networks, the creation of Jackson Hole National Monument and Redwood National Park hold special theoretical and historical significance. The creation of these park units precipitated two of the most contentious and acrimonious political battles in the history of the nation's national park and wilderness systems. Given the strong opposition that the creation of these units engendered among local economic interests and/or major timber firms, how were these areas of wilderness incorporated into the national park system? Were these parks created as a result of interest group competition and cooperation, as suggested by the pluralist model? Alternatively, were these park units created by autonomous state officials who were informed by issue networks? Further, were Jackson Hole National Monument and Redwood National Park created by economic elites operating in conjunction with policy-planning organizations? In chapter 6 I analyze the initiation and formulation of the 1990 Clean Air Act. This legislation produced the single largest expansion of environmental regulations imposed on business and industry in U.S. history.

NOTES

1. Another important view of the policymaking process is that of structural Marxism (O'Connor 1973; Poulantzas 1973; Barrow 1993, chap. 2; 2001). Currently, however, no researchers explicitly use this approach to analyze the policy areas of this study.

2. The concept of the state that I use to shape this text views the state as a collection of resources and organizational methods (Mitchell 1991).

3. McConnell argues that local economic interests dominate state and local governments (1966, chap. 6). Also, local economic interests, large agricultural concerns, large cattle interests, construction firms, and timber interests dominate land policy, agricultural policy, water development policy, and forest policy (1966, chap. 7). In addition, large corporate firms dominate those bureaucracies charged with business regulation (1966, chap. 8).

4. Almond (1988) contends that the claim of originality made by state autonomy theorists is unwarranted, because autonomous state officials have been an explicit aspect of pluralist theory from its inception.

5. The economic elite–led policy-planning network has two groupings: one characterized as "moderate" or "corporate liberal" and the other as "conservative." While these two groups will frequently compromise on issues, they sometimes cannot. When

they cannot find common ground, their struggles will usually spill over into government where each will utilize its political strength to get its way (Weinstein 1968, chap. 1; Eakins 1969, 1972; Domhoff 1978, chap. 3; 1990, 38–39; Barrow 1993, chap. 1).

6. Burch found that from 1798 to 1861, 95.8 percent of all cabinet and diplomatic appointees were drawn from economic elite circles. From 1861 to 1933, 83.5 percent of cabinet and diplomatic appointees came from elite circles. Finally, 64.4 percent of all cabinet and diplomatic appointees during the 1933–1980 period had elite backgrounds (1980/81, vol. 3, 383).

2

~

"Practical" Forestry and the U.S. Forest Service

It has been argued that the federal forest policies implemented during the Progressive era, and especially during the administration of Theodore Roosevelt, were initiated from "within the state" to control special interests, particularly corporate monopolies. Hays (1959, chap. 3) contends that forest policies adopted during the Progressive era were advocated, devised, and implemented by officials within the federal government who were aptly situated to pursue such policies. Nevertheless, he claims that these forest policies in many respects actually ran contrary to the interests of the common person, because of the scientific and professional principles guiding these officials. Klyza (1992), building on Hays's approach, argues that the development of the U.S. Forest Service during the Progressive era is consistent with state autonomy theory (Nordlinger 1981; Skowronek 1982; Skocpol 1985).[1] James Penick (1968, chap. 1), like Hays and Klyza, emphasizes the role of science in determining the content of forest policies. Closer to the issue network/state autonomy approach (Skocpol 1992), however, he holds that interest group coalitions provided the political energy for the enactment of these polices. Additionally, it is asserted that Progressive era forest policies were in response to public demands (Bates 1957).

In contrast to these positions, I argue that forest policies during the Progressive era were not based on the intersection of popular demands, pluralist politics, and the interests of autonomous officials. Instead, I contend that these policies were the outgrowth of an upper-class and corporate-based policy network promoting the use of particular forestry practices in both private and public forests in the United States.

23

THE DEVELOPMENT OF AMERICAN FORESTRY

The belief that U.S. forests were limitless was a dominant idea for most of the nineteenth century. As early as the 1860s, however, individuals began to believe that unless something was done, American forests would be exhausted (Marsh [1864] 1965; Rodgers 1991; Pisani 1997). In 1891, Congress enacted the General Land Law Revision Act, which allowed the president to set aside forests in the public domain as reserves (Steen 1997). Under this law, by 1894 Presidents Harrison and Cleveland together established forest reserves of 17.5 million acres (Sherman 1926, 130). The creation of these first forest reserves was motivated by urban and irrigation groups who saw standing forests as a means of protecting watersheds (Penick 1968, 3; White 1991, 406–7; Pisani 1996, chap. 8).

This action on the part of Congress, however, was inadequate for the sustaining of forests in the United States, since this law only affected public forests. By the late nineteenth century, four-fifths of all U.S. forests were under private control, and the remaining publicly owned forests were of relatively poor quality (Hirt 1994, xviii–xix). Many timber firms had already seen the negative effects of unmanaged exploitation in private forests located in the Upper Midwest (Robbins 1982, 4–5).

The dominant view on forests during the late nineteenth century in American academic and scientific circles emphasized forest preservation (or the nonuse of forests) and tree planting as the primary means of salvaging forests (Hays 1959, 28; McGeary 1960, 37; Pinkett 1970, 11). This view of forest lands was largely the result of the absence of a forestry profession in the United States (Smith 1938). Instead, experts on American forests were composed mostly of botanists, landscape gardeners, or other related fields. Forest preservation, in particular, ran contrary to the needs of timber firms that exploit the forests for profit. Moreover, throughout most of the nineteenth century, the dominant belief among timber manufacturers was that forestry was too "theoretically" oriented to be of practical use to commercial timber enterprises. Gifford Pinchot and others sought to modify forestry practices to make them applicable within the United States and, most important, attractive to U.S. timber firms. To achieve this objective, they developed "practical" forestry and utilized the federal government and its resources.

The Origins of American Forestry

Gifford Pinchot, a central figure in this effort, was born in 1865 to a wealthy and prominent Pennsylvania family. His paternal grandfather, Cyril C. D. Pinchot, was a wealthy merchant in Pennsylvania. Gifford Pinchot's maternal grandfather, Amos Eno, was one of the wealthiest men in New York City, while his mother, Mary (Eno) Pinchot, was a direct descendant of William Phelps, the progenitor of a family that was especially prominent during the American colonial and revolutionary period (McGeary 1960, 3; Pinkett 1970, 15, 17).

James W. Pinchot, Gifford Pinchot's father, a partner in a prosperous manufacturing firm in New York City, was an early member and a vice president of the American Forestry Association (AFA) (McGeary 1960, 4). The AFA has historically served as a policy discussion group on the issue of forests. The AFA, founded in 1875, was composed of botanists, landscape gardeners, other forest experts, estate owners, and owners and managers of timber firms and of other firms interested in forest issues (Robbins 1982, 19; Hirt 1994, 119).[2] Given James W. Pinchot's involvement in the AFA, he was in a position to know of the perils facing American forests and the need for a new approach to forest management. Moreover, the elder Pinchot had seen the work of professional foresters in Europe, where forests were treated as a crop, and their exploitation managed to provide for a sustainable yield. As a result of these factors, James encouraged his son Gifford to become a professional forester and apply European forestry principles in America. Therefore, with the encouragement and support of his father, Gifford decided to become a European trained forester and work to apply forestry practices in the United States (McGeary 1960, 4). Like most young men of his social background Gifford attended an Ivy League school—in his case, Yale. There he took courses in areas that were related to forestry, such as botany, geology, and meteorology. Like all American universities, Yale had no school of forestry at the time. Upon graduating from Yale in 1889, Pinchot traveled to Europe to study the science of forestry, where the discipline was firmly established.

In Europe his wealth and social status played a key role in gaining him access to the individuals and institutions necessary for his education as a forester. Sir Dietrich Brandis, who had introduced forest management in the government forests of British India, became Pinchot's mentor. On the advice of Brandis and other foresters, Pinchot entered the prestigious and exclusive French Forest School in Nancy. Through his relationship with Brandis while in school, Pinchot was able to have extensive visits to European forests where forestry principles had long been in practice. He was also able to meet with many of Europe's leading foresters (McGeary 1960, chap. 3; Pinkett 1970, chap. 3). Declining the advice of Brandis and other European foresters, Pinchot decided not to pursue his doctorate in France and, instead, returned to the United States in late 1890 intent on spreading and practicing the art of forestry. Upon his return from Europe, Pinchot was asked to present his views on "Government Forestry Abroad" to a joint session of the American Economic Association and the American Forestry Association (Pinkett 1970, 19–20).

In February 1892, George W. Vanderbilt, son of railroad magnate William Henry "Commodore" Vanderbilt, invited Pinchot to demonstrate the virtues of forestry practices—by managing the forests on his Biltmore estate in western North Carolina (Price 1914; Pinchot [1947] 1987, chap. 7). Pinchot was recommended to Vanderbilt by Frederick Law Olmsted, Sr., who was Vanderbilt's landscape gardener and a friend of James Pinchot (Laxton 1931, 270; Roper 1983, 418–19).[3] Olmsted, also an early member of the American Forestry Association, had suggested to Vanderbilt that his estate could be managed successfully under forestry principles (Frothingham 1941, 215; Roper 1983, 418–19).

Vanderbilt wanted the management of his forest to serve as an example of the advantages of forestry. As a stipulation of his contract with Vanderbilt, Pinchot agreed to supervise an exhibit on forestry, in conjunction with the state of North Carolina, for the Chicago World's Fair. Pinchot biographer McGeary (1960) notes, "Primarily [the exhibit] showed the accomplishments of forestry management in Europe and explained what was being done along these lines at Biltmore," and "Pinchot himself prepared a pamphlet, distributed free at the exhibit and mailed to thousands of newspapers, giving details and pictures of the first year of operations at Biltmore" (31).

By the late 1890s, Pinchot had become the leading forester for the corporate community and the upper class. Outside of Pinchot, the only other trained forester practicing forestry in the United States was working under his direction on Vanderbilt's estate. During 1894 and 1895 he expanded his work for Vanderbilt. Pinchot planned and supervised forestry operations in Vanderbilt's extensive forest holdings in North Carolina, which by 1895 encompassed one hundred thousand acres. In this same period, Pinchot was asked to examine and later manage a privately owned forest of forty thousand acres, located in the Adirondack woodlands in upstate New York and owned by railroad executive W. Seward Webb. Webb was a brother-in-law of Vanderbilt and head of the St. Lawrence and Adirondack Railway, Rutland Railroad, and Raquette Lake Railway Companies (Pinkett 1958; 1970, chap. 5; McGeary 1960, chap. 2; Pinchot 1987, chap. 11). In 1898, William C. Whitney asked Pinchot to manage his sixty-eight thousand acres of timberland, also located in the Adirondack area. Whitney served on the board of directors of the New York, Ontario and Western Railway and the Vanderbilt firm of New York, Chicago and St. Louis Railway. In addition, Whitney was the son-in-law of Henry B. Payne, a prominent Ohio economic and political figure. Payne, whose primary business was railroads, served on the board of the large Vanderbilt-dominated Lake Shore and Michigan Southern Railway. Furthermore, Whitney's brother-in-law, Oliver H. Payne, was a longtime officer and board member of Standard Oil, a Rockefeller concern. Philip Burch argues William C. Whitney "could hardly have had better business connections" (1980/81, vol. 2, 89). Also, William G. Mather, president of the Cleveland-Cliffs Iron Company, sought out Pinchot's advice on the company's extensive forest holdings in Michigan (Pinkett 1958; 1970, chap. 5; McGeary 1960, chap. 2; Pinchot 1987, 78). William Mather, who himself sat on the board of two substantial railroad companies—Wheeling and Lake Erie Railroad and the Cleveland and Pittsburgh Railroad—had a brother, Samuel, who had several important corporate connections (Burch 1980/81, vol. 2, 189 and 272–73).[4]

There was so much demand for Pinchot's time that he decided to recruit Henry Graves, a chemistry teacher and a former classmate of Pinchot's at Yale, into the field of forestry. In 1894 and 1895, Pinchot and Graves conducted a study of the white pine in central Pennsylvania and Franklin and Clinton Counties, New York, financed by D. Willis James, William E. Dodge, and Pinchot's father, James W. From this study Pinchot and Graves published *The White Pine* (1896). In the preface of *The White Pine*, Pinchot conveyed his attitude, and those of his benefactors, toward forestry during this early period:

> The motive which gave rise to this attempt [to study the white pine], in the minds of all those who have shared in the work, was the desire to assist in making clear the real nature of forestry, in exciting an interest in the subjects with which it deals, in stimulating others to similar research, and, above all, in facilitating and hastening the general introduction of right methods of forest management, by which alone our forests can be saved. (Pinchot and Graves 1896, vii)

In short, this policy network's objective during this period was the spreading of forestry practices throughout the United States. This objective is also reflected in the publicity surrounding Pinchot's work on Vanderbilt's estate.

The number of experts trained in forestry practices was substantially expanded after the establishment of the Yale School of Forestry in 1900. It was the first school in the country to offer an advanced degree in forestry, and it dominated the field for decades. Gifford Pinchot and his family took the lead in its establishment by collectively contributing $150,000 to open the school and an additional $150,000 over the years. James Pinchot also allowed the school to conduct its summer school and fieldwork in his Gray Towers estate, located in Milford, Pennsylvania (McGeary 1960, 48–49). Timber magnate Frederick E. Weyerhaeuser served as chairperson to a group (Hidy et. al. 1963, 300), formed in 1905, that led an industry-wide effort that raised $100,000 to establish a Chair of Lumbering in the Yale Forestry School. Russell Sage's widow and Andrew Carnegie each matched this sum with $100,000 ("Lumberman and Lumber Journals" 1910, 381).[5] Gifford Pinchot's protégé, Henry Graves, was made the school's first dean.

As indicated by the class backgrounds, and the class connections, of the members of the policy network that developed and financed forestry in the United States, it was members of the economic elite who imported forestry into the country. Despite the efforts of this corporate and upper-class policy network, however, forestry was still a fledgling in the United States in the late 1890s. It would take this network's use of the state's resources to firmly establish forestry in the United States, both in the private sector and the public forest reserves.

The National Forest Commission

While the federal government had created forest reserves within the public
domain in 1891, it had not provided for the protection or management of
those reserves. The reserves were under the jurisdiction of the Department of
the Interior, while the Division of Forestry was located in the Department of
Agriculture. This bureaucratic fragmentation meant that unrestricted grazing
continued in the reserves as did unauthorized logging. In 1894, the American
Forestry Association petitioned Congress and the president about the "neces-
sity of an immediate and thorough inquiry into the scientific, commercial, cli-
matic, and economic bearings of the forestry question . . . to establish a sys-
tematic and permanent policy concerning the national forests" (as quoted in
Pinkett 1970, 38). That same year, Pinchot and Dr. Charles S. Sargent agreed
to lobby Congress to create a commission to study and report on the forests
in the public domain. Dr. Sargent, an outspoken advocate for preservation (or
nonuse) of the federal forests, was a professor of arboriculture and director of
the Arnold Arboretum at Harvard University. He was also publisher of the
journal *Garden and Forest.* As part of this lobbying effort, Pinchot went to the
New York Chamber of Commerce and the New York Board of Trade and
Transportation and received their support for the creation of a forest commission (Pinchot 1987, 47).

In 1896, largely in response to the efforts of Sargent and Pinchot, Secretary
of the Interior Hoke Smith called on the National Academy of Sciences to
form a commission to report on the "inauguration of a rational forest policy"
for the forests of the public domain (as quoted in Pinkett 1970, 39). This commission came into being despite the opposition of the then-head of the
Forestry Division, Bernhard Fernow. Fernow believed that the creation of a
commission would undermine pending legislation that would have established
some level of management over the public forests (Rodgers 1991, 220). The
commission, known popularly as the National Forest Commission, was composed, with the exception of Pinchot, of members from the National Academy
of Sciences. Sargent was its chairman; Pinchot, its secretary (Pinchot 1987,
91–92).[6]

The commission was divided from the start, with Pinchot on one side and
Sargent on the other. Sargent, reflecting the dominant thought on forests in
the academic community, pushed for a policy that called for preservation (or
nonuse) of the forests in the public domain, while Pinchot argued for the managed usage of the national forests. Among the commission, Pinchot was in the
minority. Specifically, it rejected Pinchot's recommendation that its study
should be guided by forestry principles (McGeary 1960, 40–41; Pinchot 1987,
chap. 16).

On 3 June 1897, while the commission still was deliberating, Congress
passed the Forest Management Act.[7] An amendment to this legislation called

for the "management, preservation, and use of existing and future reserves" (as quoted in McGeary 1960, 41). As a result of this amendment, the day after the passage of the Forest Management Act, Secretary of the Interior Cornelius N. Bliss offered Pinchot the position of special agent for the Interior Department. Pinchot (1987) describes his duties as special agent as follows:

> I was to examine and report upon the suspended Reserves, their condition and needs, their forests, and their relations to lumbering, agriculture, mining, grazing, commerce, and settlement. I was to draw up a set of principles to govern future increase and decrease in the Reserves and apply them to individual cases. Finally, I was to report a practicable plan for the establishment of a Forest Service, with specific recommendations for individual Reserves—*recommendations which the report of the Commission had not contained* [emphasis added]. (123)

The significance of Pinchot's appointment to this key position was not lost on Sargent. According to McGeary (1960), "The Commission's chairman [Sargent] evidently felt that Pinchot had turned traitor by accepting a strategic post where he could see that his own ideas rather than those presented in the Commission's report would prevail" (42).

Why was Pinchot given this position? Pinchot (1987, 131) himself attributes his appointment to his membership on the commission. This explanation, however, is inadequate. He was one of seven members who served on the commission and, as already noted, the only one who was not a member of the National Academy of Sciences. Pinchot's biographers ascribe his appointment to the fact that he was the first American who had received formal training as a forester (McGeary 1960; Pinkett 1970).

His appointment, however, merits further examination. Pinchot did not have an advanced degree, and he concedes that Henry Graves by this time was a better-trained forester than he was (Pinchot 1987, 72). Furthermore, individuals like Sargent, while not trained in "forestry," were considered experts on forests and had several years of training and experience in the area. Sargent had published in 1884 a notable and widely read report on forests entitled "Report on the Forests of North America," which, in historian Andrew Rodgers III's (1991) words, brought Sargent "instantaneous acclaim" (32–34). Sir Dietrich Brandis described Sargent as the foremost expert on American forests. Brandis wrote the following to Pinchot in a letter:

> Sargent has fought the battle of Forestry in the U.S. for more than 20 years, if ever Forestry is to be reality in your country, his work in publishing the "Silva" and otherwise, will always be recognized as having laid the foundation of an accurate knowledge of American trees. You have several times in your letters complained of his obstinacy and I have always advised you to keep on good terms with him. (1897 August 9)

In contrast, Pinchot, who at the time of his appointment was thirty-one years old, had worked on the issue of forests for only seven years. Moreover, Pinchot held a view on forest management that was contrary to that of the government's own commission on forest management. Therefore, in bypassing Sargent, and the other preservationists, the secretary of the interior, and later the secretary of agriculture, chose to ignore the most developed scientific discourse on forests in the United States. Instead, they chose a view on forests whose adherents were relatively lacking in training, but, as described below, was consistent with the U.S. timber industry's policy preferences.

PINCHOT AS CHIEF FORESTER

Between 1886 and 1898, the Agriculture Department's Forestry Division was headed by Dr. Bernhard Fernow, a graduate of the Prussian Forest School at Muenden. After working in the Prussian State Forest Department, Fernow became a founder of the American Forestry Association and served as its secretary for many years (Rodgers 1991, chaps. 2 and 3). When Fernow resigned to take up an offer to organize the new forestry school at Cornell University, the secretary of agriculture offered the position to Pinchot. Pinchot became head of the Division of Forestry on 1 July 1898, shortly after he submitted his report to the secretary of the interior.

Two of Pinchot's predecessors, Franklin B. Hough (who served from 1881 through 1886) and Fernow, had attempted to introduce European forestry to American forests, but they were hampered by the division's meager appropriations (Rodgers 1991, 58 and chap. 3). From 1883 to 1890, for example, the division was appropriated $10,000 annually, $2,000 for salaries and $8,000 for investigations (Rodgers 1991, 145). Moreover, Fernow advocated the creation of forest reserves in the public domain and their management according to forestry principles. Fernow supported legislation to achieve these goals throughout his tenure (Rodgers 1991, chaps. 3, 4, and 5).

As head of the Division of Forestry, Pinchot had three objectives. First, he sought to use the division to expand the number of privately owned forests that utilized forestry techniques. Pinchot also aimed to use the division as a means to expand the number of foresters trained in "practical forestry." Finally, he wanted to apply forestry principles to the federal forest reserves. He concluded that this final objective could only be attained with the transfer of the forest reserves from the General Land Office in the Department of the Interior to his division in the Department of Agriculture. This transfer would require an act of Congress.

Expanding Private Use of "Practical" Forestry

After only three months at the Division of Forestry, Pinchot issued Circular 21. The policy derived from the circular offered to owners of timberland assistance in establishing forestry practices, including "working plans for conservative lumbering, with full directions for practical work, and assistance on the ground" (Pinchot 1987, 141). For owners of small tracts of timber, this help was offered for free. Owners of larger tracts of timberland, such as timber firms, were required to pay the expenses of the division's assistants, but not their salaries, and the costs of local assistants.

Pinchot (1987) later wrote of this program that "this was our major offensive," and it quickly proved successful (141). The management assistance program substantially expanded the usage of forestry practices among private forests. Within a year of the promulgation of Circular 21, 123 owners of timberland requested the division's aid in establishing forestry practices on their land. In ten years, the division received 938 formal requests for management assistance on thirteen million acres. In total, it surveyed eight million acres of privately owned forests. These lands, which laid mostly in large timber tracts and were owned by large timber owners, constituted a substantial portion of the productive forests in the United States. The large timber owners participating in the program included industrialist and banker J. P. Morgan, William G. Rockefeller (the brother of John D. Rockefeller), railroad magnate Abram S. Hewitt, railroad magnate E. H. Harriman,[8] the Northern Pacific Railroad, the Kirby Lumber Company of Texas, the Great Northern Paper Company, the Moose River Lumber Company, and the Weyerhaeuser Timber Company (Pinkett 1958, 47; 1970, 48–49; Hays 1959, 29; Robbins 1982, 30).

The division's assistance program helped educate the public and timber owners of the feasibility and desirability of forestry. According to Ralph Hosmer (1945), at the time a young forester in the Division of Forestry, the management assistance program "carried forestry from the office and the lecture hall into the woods and demonstrated that the forester was a man whose business it was to produce successive crops of timber trees. In effect it inaugurated extension forestry in the United States" (559).

As requests came into the Division of Forestry for assistance under its management assistance program, the division required more personnel and other organizational resources in order to satisfy the increasing demands. Congress responded to the division's needs with substantial budgetary increases. When Pinchot took over the division, it had an annual budget of $29,000 and eleven employees. Over the next five years, the division received budgetary increases of 70, 82.4, 109.4, 57.3, and 28.5 percent. When its status was elevated to that of a bureau in 1901, it had 179 employees (McGeary 1960, 52). By the end of the fiscal year 1903–1904, the last full year of the Circular 21 program, the Bureau of Forestry had a total budget of $312,000 and had 307 employees (U.S. Department of Agriculture 1904, 307 and 316). According to a 1908 report by the secretary of agriculture, most of the budgetary growth that the division, and later the bureau, experienced during this early period was expended on Pinchot's Circular 21 program (U.S. Department of Agriculture 1909, 78).

Hence, contrary to the claims of state autonomists, bureaucratic growth is not necessarily indicative of autonomy (Skowronek 1982; Klyza 1992, 186). In the case of the Division of Forestry, its growth resulted from a program that subsidized the timber industry by providing it the expertise needed to improve management and profitability at no or low cost. If the division had ceased to serve the interests of this industry, its budget and bureaucratic structure would have been reduced. This is consistent with Hirt's (1994) finding that in the post–World War II period, it was that portion of the forest service's budget subsidizing timber firms' harvesting activities in the national forest that experienced the greatest growth and political stability. In contrast, other budgetary requests made by the forest service were often ignored and suffered from political uncertainty.

With increasing resources at his disposal, Pinchot was able to help shape the future of the profession of American forestry. This meant not only supplanting the previously dominant American academic thought on forests but limiting the influence of European foresters, with whom he disagreed with over the practice of forestry in United States.[9] Writing in his autobiography on the bureau's need for trained foresters, Pinchot (1987) argued:

> Of course any number of foresters from abroad were ready to come over. But my experience with Schenck [a German forester who worked under him on Vanderbilt's estate] and Mlodzianshky [a foreign-trained forester within the division] was not encouraging. I was perfectly certain it would be worse than useless to fill the gap with imported Europeans, even if we had the money to import them, and in that I was perfectly right. (147)

Pinchot (1987) goes on to add, "We had small confidence in the leadership of Dr. Fernow or Dr. Schenck. We distrusted them and their German lack of faith in American Forestry. What we wanted was American foresters trained by Americans in American ways for the work ahead in American forests" (152). Pinchot manifested his disagreement with European foresters as early as 1899 when in an address to the Yale student body concerning the future of the profession of forestry in the United States, he declared, "It would be easily possible . . . to secure Germans or other foreigners [to fill the personnel needs of the Division of Forestry], but a considerable experience has convinced me that . . . the attempt to use foreign-born men trained abroad is not likely to succeed" (1899, 157).

Pinchot's dislike of European foresters stemmed from the fact that European forestry emphasized data collection and the intensive management of forests, while Pinchot's idea of forestry emphasized profit making and the management of large tracts of land with a minimum amount of labor. Referring to the differences between forestry in theory and forestry in practice, Pinchot stated that "they are not even kissing kin" (as quoted in Hidy et al. 1963, 137).

Pinchot was not the only one that regarded European forestry as too "academically" oriented. Fernow was criticized because much of the work he wished to institute in the Division of Forestry was considered to be too "theoretical." Rodgers (1991) documents that Fernow acknowledged his detractors:

> "I hear," wrote Fernow, "some 'practical' engineers say that in practice it would be impossible to apply such refined knowledge, and hence the test data should refer to conditions only which occur or are usual and recognizable in actual practice." This was the sharp issue of "pure versus practical science." (231)

With respect to forestry, the perceived division between pure and practical science created in the American lexicon the term *practical forestry*. This form of forestry is considered "practical" because it is viewed as consistent with the profit motive of timber firms. Practical forestry is, in the American mind, contrary to "theoretical forestry," which was strongly associated with European or German forestry practices. In his 1914 speech to the graduating Yale class, Fernow acknowledged the putative dichotomy between German or theoretical forestry and American or practical forestry (Rodgers 1991, 537).

Prior to the efforts of Pinchot and others, the view of forestry as overly theoretical and therefore not useful to timber firms was dominant in the timber industry. As a result of his work in the field Henry Graves (1901) concluded, "The fact that forestry is scientific has proved a serious obstacle in the way of its adoption by many forest owners in this country. Lumbermen have a strong prejudice against scientific foresters, for they believe the latter are theorists and that they can offer nothing practical" (105). Frederick Weyerhaeuser, son of timber magnate George Weyerhaeuser, at the American Forest Congress of 1905, argued that there was the perception in the timber industry that forestry was incompatible with the profit motive of the timber firm. He pointed out:

> Practical forestry ought to be of more interest and importance to lumberman than to any other class of men. Unfortunately, they have not always appreciated this fact. There has been a firmly rooted idea that forestry was purely theoretical and incapable of application in a business way. (American Forestry Association 1905, 137)

The reason that European forestry was viewed as too theoretical by the U.S. timber industry was because it treated the issue of profit as a secondary concern, emphasizing instead the integrity of forests. This emphasis reflected the political and environmental conditions in which European forestry developed. As Samuel Dana and Sally Fairfax (1980) note, in Europe "land was scarce, trees were correspondingly scarce, and yet they appeared to be virtually indispensable to the nation's life, economy, defense, and survival" (152). Reflective of these factors, many of Western and Central Europe's most productive forests were under government control. It is under these environmental and political conditions that

European foresters and government policymakers prioritized the viability of forests over profit making. As Dana and Fairfax point out, "German foresters developed a technique for managing forests under conditions of scarcity, stability, and certainty" (52). In the United States, however, forests were vast and timber was in apparent abundance. Furthermore, timber firms managed forests, and harvested timber, to produce profit, and they had no use for a form of forestry that subsumed profit under the goal of forest maintenance.

One of the most forceful and direct expressions of the need for forestry to submit to the profit motive of the timber industry was made by Henry Graves.[10] In an article entitled "The Study and Practice of Silviculture," Graves wrote, shortly after assuming the directorship of the Yale School of Forestry, that the success of forestry in America depended on the ability of the forestry profession to demonstrate to the owners of timber firms the compatibility of forestry with profitability.

> A demonstration of silviculture [the science of forest cultivation], which pretends to a demonstration of practical forestry, but which makes financial considerations of incidental interest alone, does an injustice to forestry, especially at this time when the science is on trial as really practical for business men. (1901, 108)

In the same article, Graves admonishes those in the profession of forestry that their conception of the science of forestry must actively incorporate and prioritize the timber firm's profit motive:

> The measures, which the forester as silviculturist would like to use, are modified by financial considerations. The silviculturist must expect always to fall short of his ideal. He must always make some sacrifices and his final method must always be a compromise between what would produce the most perfect results silviculturally and what is possible for the owner financially. (109)

Graves further admonishes foresters, "No greater mistake can be made than to assume an uncompromising attitude in the face of financial considerations and public opinion and to insist that measures must be used which involve more money than the owner can afford to expend" (109). Finally, he notifies European-trained foresters:

> The forest owners demand more here than abroad. . . . The forester who expects to accomplish at once the results secured in Europe will fail. The American forester must devise systems of management which will accomplish the owner's object and at the same time maintain the productiveness of the forest. (109)

During the post–World War II period, nontimber views of forests grew in popularity. In particular, the public at large began to value forests for the recreational opportunities they offered, as well as for their intrinsic value as a home for wildlife (Hays 1987, 1997, 1998; Sellers 1999). The U.S. forestry profession, however, was impervious to these novel views and continued to conceptualize forests primarily as timber-producing, and hence profit-producing, resources (Twight and Lyden 1989; Twight, Lyden, and Tuchmann 1990; Hirt 1994).

The Establishment of Practical Forestry

The corporate and upper-class forest policy network, using its own resources and those of the Division of Forestry, sought to expand the number of individuals trained in American or practical forestry. It is within this context of shaping the course of the profession of forestry in America that Pinchot and his family, as well as others, endowed the School of Forestry at Yale. As already pointed out, Henry Graves, as dean of the Yale Forest School, put a priority on the financial aspects of forestry practices.[11] In 1899, the Division of Forestry instituted a program that enticed American college students into its service. Students accepted into this program would be given the title of "student assistant" and paid $25 a month, plus expenses, for fieldwork and $40 a month for work in Washington by the Division of Forestry (Pinchot 1987, 147). From Pinchot's early recruiting efforts, Overton W. Price, Ralph Hosmer, William L. Hall, and Raphael Zon, all of whom later played important leadership roles in forest conservation, were brought into the Division of Forestry (Pinkett 1970, 51).

In 1900, Pinchot led in the organization of the Society of American Foresters. He served as its president from 1900 to 1908 and again in 1910–1911 (Pinkett 1970, 87). Pinchot biographer and historian, Harold Pinkett, noted in 1970:

> The Society has grown into a vibrant organization that has achieved the purpose of its founders with conspicuous success. Its unity of fellowship is notable in public and private forest work and it has long been acknowledged as the principal spokesman of the profession of forestry in the United States and a leading force in the standardization of instruction in the nation's forest schools. (87)

In 1940, after listing the various contributions the society had made to building forestry education in the United States, Ralph S. Hosmer (1940), who served twenty-eight years as head of Cornell's forestry department, concluded that "the Society of American Foresters has thus had a profound influence on the shaping of the curricula of all the schools of forestry in America" (854). The society continues to be responsible for granting accreditation to forestry schools.

Pinchot also sought to help shape American thought on forestry during his tenure as head of the Division of Forestry through the Collaborator program. Under this program, certain academic and scientific professionals were put on retainer for $300 a year, and their ideas on forestry issues were published

"under Government auspices." By 1901, the division had twenty-five Collab-
orators on retainer (Pinchot 1987, 149–50).

The efforts of individuals such as Graves, Pinchot, George Vanderbilt (who
planned that his estate would serve as an example of the compatibility of
forestry practices and profitability [Laxton 1931, 269]), Frederick Law Olmsted, and Pinchot's other benefactors to make forestry more attractive to timber capitalists led to its acceptance by the timber industry. J. E. Defebaugh,
editor of the *American Lumberman,* and N. W. McLeod, president of the
National Lumber Manufacturers' Association, both attested to the acceptance
of practical forestry by the timber industry. Furthermore, both attributed this
acceptance to the fact that forestry became sensitive to the profit motive of the
timber firms. Defebaugh spoke at the American Forest Congress of 1905.
Here he gave a speech entitled "The Changed Attitude of Lumbermen toward
Forestry," in which he argued that:

> There has been a change of heart within recent years on the part of American
> lumbermen toward the forestry idea there can be no doubt. If you should ask me
> to what I ascribe this sentiment I would say that the most important step forward
> was made by the disciples of forestry when they ceased to preach the doctrine of
> indirect and deferred benefits and began to demonstrate that direct benefits could
> be made to result from forestry as a science and as a practice. (American Forestry
> Association 1905, 115)

McLeod also spoke at this congress, crediting the Bureau of Forestry, under Pinchot, with molding forestry into a discipline that is useful to the timber industry:

> Such an assemblage as the one before me would have been quite impossible ten
> years ago. [The American Forest Congress of 1905 was attended by several tim-
> ber industry representatives and forestry experts (American Forestry Association
> 1905, 452–72).] The lumberman and the forester were then far apart. So long as
> forestry was regarded as merely scientific, but little progress was made; but as it
> came largely through the influence of our Bureau of Forestry, to be more clearly
> understood as a [b]usiness matter, the prospect has brightened rapidly. . . . *In
> developing an American system of forestry founded upon sound business principles* and
> adapted to local conditions, the Bureau of Forestry is doing a very important work
> [emphasis added]. (American Forestry Association 1905, 99)

McLeod went on to explain that "the Bureau [of Forestry] has in a large measure succeeded in convincing the lumbermen that forestry is not antagonistic
to the lumbermen's interest, but in line with it" (American Forestry Association 1905, 99).

The funding of the Yale School of Forestry by the timber industry, as
explained earlier, serves as further evidence of the support within the industry

for practical forestry. In addition, as discussed later, the industry's support for the transfer of the federal forest reserves to the jurisdiction of the Bureau of Forestry also demonstrates support for practical forestry.

Transfer of the Forest Reserves

Pinchot's goal of transferring the forest reserves from the Interior Department to the Agriculture Department was supported by both Presidents William McKinley (Hays 1959, 39; McGeary 1960, 53; Robbins 1982, 31) and Theodore Roosevelt. Pinchot's influence with Roosevelt, as both close friend and political adviser (McGeary 1960; Pinkett 1970), was seen in Roosevelt's endorsement of the transfer in his very first message to Congress as president in 1901 (Hays 1959, 29; McGeary 1960, 54). Yet this presidential support was not enough to induce congressional action; a wider lobbying campaign was needed.

The American Forestry Association joined the campaign early, passing a resolution expressing support for placing the public forests under the authority of the Division of Forestry (McGeary 1960, 59). Many cattle "barons," hoping that the Division of Forestry could bring order to the grazing practices of the public forests, supported the transfer to the Department of Agriculture, and their American National Livestock Association began adopting resolutions endorsing the idea in 1901. The American Mining Congress also passed similar resolutions (Hays 1959, 41–42; Penick 1968, 4–5). In 1904–1905, the corporate community was mobilized to demonstrate its support for the transfer idea. Under the auspices of the American Forestry Association, of which Pinchot had been a member since his Yale days, the American Forest Congress was organized in Washington, D.C. It was organized by the Committee of Arrangements, which had among its members the presidents of the Pennsylvania and Northern Pacific Railroads, as well as the presidents of the National Lumber Manufacturers, Live Stock, and Irrigation Associations. Also on this committee were Frederick Weyerhaeuser, of the Weyerhaeuser timber family, and R. A. Long, the president of the Southern Lumber Manufacturers Association (American Forestry Association 1905, v–vi).

The congress was organized for the explicit purpose of demonstrating support for the transfer of the forest reserves to the Department of Agriculture (Pinchot 1987, 254). Held in early January 1905, it had among its delegates "influential foresters, lumbermen, miners, railroad men, wool growers, and men representing the grazing and irrigation interests" (McGeary 1960, 60). Several lumber-related trade associations, such as the National Wholesale Lumber Dealers' Association, the Retail Lumber Dealers' Association, the National Lumber Manufacturers' Association, Pacific Coast Lumbermen, the Southern Lumber Manufacturers' Association, and the Mississippi Valley Lumber Association, sent representatives to the congress (American Forestry Association 1905, 452–72). The presence of railroad representatives at the congress was especially significant, because the federal government, as a means of financing railroad development, had given vast tracts of forests and other public lands to railroad firms. Railroads represented at the American Forest Congress included the Chicago and Northwestern Railroad Company, the Norfolk and Western Railway, the Erie Railroad Company, the Northern Pacific Railroad, the Baltimore and Ohio Railroad, the Burlington and Quincy Railway Company, the Missouri, Kansas and Texas Railway system, the Cleveland, Cincinnati, Chicago and St. Louis Railway Company, the Union Pacific Railroad, and the Southern Pacific Railroad (American Forestry Association 1905, 452–72). On 1 February 1905, within a month of the closing of the American Forest Congress, the U.S. Congress enacted legislation authorizing the transfer of the forest reserves to the Bureau of Forestry in the Department of Agriculture.

The embracing of practical forestry by the timber industry and railroad firms, and the support they gave to the transfer of the federal forest reserves to the Bureau of Forestry, was predicated on two factors. It was evident that forestry practices could help ensure a future supply of timber. In addition, the application of scientific forestry on the private and public forests placed upward pressure on timber prices. As William Graf (1990) describes, the market conditions facing timber firms during the 1890s were not favorable:

> Throughout the West the lumber market was in disarray. During the 1890s, real lumber prices declined as more timber was harvested. In order to maintain profits, companies cut increased amounts to make up in volume what was lacking in unit price. This strategy further depressed prices by glutting the market so that wasteful cutting practices and anticonservation positions made short-term economic sense. No operator could afford to wait until tomorrow to cut what he could today. (114)

The application of practical forestry to private forests and the national forests helped stabilize timber prices for two reasons. First, forestry practices require a slow down of timber production. Second, the application of forestry to the expanding national forests helped stabilize timber prices by limiting competition from small independent operators.[12] With the Bureau of Forestry, later the U.S. Forest Service (in 1905), strictly regulating access and production in the national forests, small operators who had been dependent on the public lands for timber were driven out of business (White 1991, 409). Under Pinchot's and Roosevelt's auspices, the national forests expanded to approximately 195 million acres (Sherman 1926, 130 and 132). Furthermore, with the federal forest reserves managed according to practical forestry principles and not preservation precepts, large timber firms could have access to these reserves when and if needed.

Prior to World War II, the timber industry did ask the forest service to refrain from producing timber from the national forests to lessen the saturation of the market, and the service complied (Robbins 1982, 71; White 1991, 409; Hirt 1994, 54). As demand grew for timber in the postwar period, however, the service made the national forests increasingly available to the timber industry (Hirt 1994). In addition, the forest service has historically subsidized the timber industry in its efforts to extract timber from the national forests. These policies continued into the 1990s (O'Toole 1988; Hirt 1994; U.S. General Accounting Office 1995, 1998; Baden and O'Brien 1997).

Therefore, because the service restricted access to the national forests, its growth and development during this early period can be most aptly interpreted as a subsidy to large timber firms. By 1908, the forest service employed a total of 2,753 individuals, and it had an annual budget of approximately $3.7 million (U.S. Department of Agriculture 1909, 410 and 775). Of this sum, approximately $2.5 million was expended on the "administration and protection" of the national forests. Another $600,000 was spent on "permanent improvements" (i.e., roads and permanent structures, such as barracks for employees and administrative buildings) (U.S. Department of Agriculture 1909, 409).

THE UTILITARIAN POLICY NETWORK

There is a consensus among historians who study the politics of conservation during the Progressive era that the policies associated with the creation and management of the national forests neither undermined the interests of big business nor served the mass public's economic interests (Hays 1959, 32–33; McGeary 1960, 85; Penick 1968, 35–39; Robbins 1982; Graf 1990, 114; White 1991, 406–9). Despite the role that conservation policies played in raising timber prices, and hence their derivative products (e.g., paper and wood), and in undermining the economic position of small timber operators, no effective or sustained network arose to oppose the spreading of conservation practices or their application to the national forests. Elmo R. Richardson (1962), who conducted the most extensive study of opponents to conservation policies during the Progressive era, found that two organizations were created for the explicit purpose of opposing conservation policies. These organizations, the National Domain League and the Western Conservation League, specifically called for the ceding of the public domain to the states. Richardson (1962) offers the following description of these organizations and their relative ineffectiveness: "Neither of these organizations was notably successful as a publicity bureau. Both lacked enough active participants and were limited in finances and facilities. Their intermittent communications must have converted very few people who were not already in the ranks of the critics" (91). Graf (1990), another historian of opposition to conservation and environmental policies, argues that the National Public Domain League and the Western Conservation League "led short, fruitless lives that generated little heat and even less light in the controversies beyond newspaper copy and self-aggrandizement for their few participants" (130–31).

While the opposition to conservation policies, or the utilitarian policy network, lacked effective organization as well as credible spokespersons, the practical forestry policy network was very aggressive with the message that conservation policies served the public good and were antimonopoly in orientation. Pinchot (1987) believed that the American "Forest Congress was a powerful influence not only toward securing the transfer [of the forest reserves], but also in spreading sound knowledge and wise conclusions about Forestry throughout the length and breadth of America" (254). Furthermore, in addition to his early publications touting forestry, Pinchot, through the forest service, mounted an expensive public relations campaign designed to "educate" the public on the benefits of practical forestry. Pinkett (1970) briefly lists and describes the various means that Pinchot used as head of the forest service to preach the gospel of forestry:

> As head of the Forest Service he conducted an extensive and varied publicity program designed to acquaint the populace with the need for forest conservation and development . . . . The program included the furnishing of technical information to individuals, on the ground or by correspondence; preparation and distribution of publications; public addresses; loan and sale of lantern slides, pictures, and other illustrative material for the use of lecturers, writers, and other persons; cooperation with teachers and preparation of officials in educational work; exhibits at expositions; and preparation of official information concerning forestry in brief statements given to newspapers and magazines for publication. (81)

In 1908, for example, the service expended approximately $56,000 on the "diffusion of information" (U.S. Department of Agriculture 1909, 409). After reviewing Pinchot's publicity efforts as chief forester, Stephen Ponder (1987) concludes:

> His aggressive use of government resources to present his perceptions of conservation policy to commercial newspapers and magazines in a form acceptable as news allowed Pinchot to dominate discussion of natural resources management at the beginning of the twentieth century and to influence those discussions down to the present.[13] (35)

Three major conferences were held to promote the value of the conservation of natural resources. In addition to facilitating the transfer of the forest reserves, the American Forest Congress of 1905 brought positive attention to the issue of forest conservation (Pinchot 1987, chap. 62). In the spring of 1908, the Conference of Governors was held to discuss and promote the management and conservation of natural resources. Joining all the governors and various other government officials at the conference, as well as labor leader John Mitchell and populist leader William Jennings Bryan, were industry leaders. Among these representatives of business and industry were steel magnate Andrew Carnegie, John Hayes Hammond,[14] James J. Hill, president of the Northern Pacific Railroad, lumberman R. A. Long, and H. A. Jastrow, president of the National Livestock Association.[15] All of them gave speeches in support of the conservation of natural resources (Pinchot 1987, chap. 64). Also, in February 1909, Pinchot organized and chaired the North American Conservation Conference. This conference was composed largely of public officials from Canada, Mexico, and the United States. Pinchot had also begun to organize a World Conservation Conference, to be held in September 1909, when President Taft killed the idea (Pinchot 1987, chap. 65).

CONCLUSION

In the evolution of forest conservation, there were several key points of intersection between members of the economic elite and the development of forest policies. Pinchot's training in Europe and his attainment of professional prominence were the result of his own and his patrons' wealth and status. Therefore, the idea of establishing practical forestry in the United States was developed and promoted within the upper class and corporate community. Second, the transfer of the national forests to the jurisdiction of the forest service was accomplished through the mobilization of big business support. Third, a policy network, led by economic elites, intervened directly to mold the profession of forestry into a discipline that served the needs of the U.S. timber industry.[16]

This last intervention by economic elites has the widest ramifications for both the profession of forestry and state theory. It might be argued that the form the forestry profession ultimately took was the result of the structural needs of the economy (Poulantzas 1973; O'Connor 1973; Barrow 1993, chap. 2; 2001). If the National Forest Commission is to be taken as any indication, however, the U.S. academic and scientific communities resisted the development and application of practical forestry. As a result, Pinchot, while head of the Division of Forestry, was forced to hire individuals, many of whom were still in college, with little or no training in forestry or in related fields. It was not until Pinchot, and other members of the economic elite, funded the School of Forestry at Yale did the U.S. timber industry, as well as the federal government, have foresters well trained in the principles of practical forestry.

Furthermore, the development of practical forestry lends support to Domhoff's (1990, 51) contention that intellectuals are a resource for members of the economic elite. With the dissatisfaction of the timber industry with existing forest and forestry experts, it bypassed these people. Instead, economic elites patronized and helped develop experts whose approach to forests and forest management was consistent with the industry's views. Moreover, the bypassing of the American preservationists, and the European foresters, lends support to Domhoff's (1990, 51) argument that in regards to the operation of policy networks and public policy development it is not enough for scientific experts or intellectuals to take a "class-neutral" approach to an issue, as argued by state autonomy theorist Theda Skocpol (1986/87). Instead, the rise to prominence of practical forestry suggests that economic elites seek out and successfully promote those intellectuals and experts whose advice conforms with their outlook and preferences.

Additionally, despite the fact that federal forest policies ran contrary to the economic interests of most consumers and small timber producers, the public as a whole remained quiescent. The inability of the public to oppose the institution of forest policies can in part be attributed to the symbols and rhetoric disseminated through the publicity campaign undertaken by Pinchot and others.

NOTES

1. For a specific critique of Klyza's (1992) argument, see Gonzalez (1998).

2. Writing about the American Forestry Association in the 1950s, Hirt points out that timber "industry advertisements heavily supported the AFA's magazine, *American Forests*, and industry leaders enjoyed significant representation on the AFA's board and among its membership" (1994, 119).

3. Both James Pinchot and Olmsted had several discussions on the issue of forests and the need for the application of forestry principles in the United States (Rodgers 1991, 170).

4. Samuel Mather was a longtime high official in the Ohio iron ore concern of Picklands, Mather & Co., and he was a director of Morgan-dominated U.S. Steel. He was also an active board member on almost all major Cleveland banks and a director of the large Lackawanna Steel Co. Additionally, Mather served on the executive committee of the National Civic Federation, which Burch (1980/81) describes as "a heavily business-weighted body [that] represented something approaching a politico-economic establishment in the first part of the [twentieth] century" (vol. 2, 149–50).

5. Russell Sage was a partner of railroad magnate Jay Gould (Burch 1980/81, vol. 2, 70).

6. For a full list of the commission's members see Pinchot (1987, 91–92).

7. This act was part of the Sundry Appropriations Bill for that year and is also known as the Pettigrew amendment.

8. Harriman's most substantial holding was the Union Pacific Railroad.

9. For example, Pinchot's mentor, Brandis, criticized much of Pinchot's early forestry work and the bureau's work implemented under its management assistance program. He felt the bureau's work, in particular, lacked detail and was applied in a largely wholesale manner (Pinkett 1958, 48; 1970, 49). Fernow also criticized Pinchot's early forestry work (Pinchot 1987, 73).

10. Graves became head of the U.S. Forest Service in 1910.

11. In 1929, Graves was made cochair of a committee entitled Forest Education

Inquiry. The committee was under the auspices of the Society of American Foresters. With a grant of $30,000 from the Carnegie Corporation, the Forest Education Inquiry endeavored "to aid in strengthening the foundations of the system of forest education in America" (as quoted in Hosmer 1940). According to forest conservation leader Ralph Hosmer (1940), under the committee:

> For two years an exhaustive study was carried on. Every school of forestry in the United States was visited. Innumerable conferences were held with those employing foresters, questionnaires were filled by the alumni of all the schools, masses of data were collected, tabulated, and analyzed. All phases of the problem were considered.

This effort yielded in 1932 a book entitled *Forest Education*, coauthored by Graves and Professor Cedric H. Guise.

12. By the early 1910s, timber prices reached a peak (Hidy et al. 1963, 308).

13. For a discussion of how Gifford Pinchot's efforts in the area of natural resource management continue to affect the American public's conception of natural resources, see Taylor (1992).

14. Burch (1980/81) points out that John Hayes "Hammond was . . . president of the Esperanza Mining Co., vice-president of the Guanajuato Power & Electric Co., and a director of the big Utah Copper Co. and the Guggenheim Exploration Co., a family-controlled firm that had a substantial interest in a number of noteworthy enterprises, including the Yukon Gold Co." Hammond was also a member of the National Civic Federation (vol. 2, 195–96).

15. Later in 1908, James J. Hill, John Hayes Hammond, and Andrew Carnegie would all serve on the National Conservation Commission. This commission's purpose was to take full inventory of the nation's natural resources (Pinchot 1987, 356).

16. Barrow (1990) provides an excellent study of how business influence was used to shape the American university. Much of his discussion focuses on how this influence was used to shape the academic disciplines of economics, psychology, and political science during the Progressive era.

3

~

The Political Economy of the
National Park System

In the preceding chapter I demonstrated how the U.S. Forest Service and its professional precepts were shaped by an economic elite–led policy-planning network. In this chapter I analyze how another "strong" agency within the federal government, the National Park Service, was shaped by economic elites to the general benefit of the corporate community. A strong government agency is one that has centralized management, ample resources, and a professional staff (Skocpol 1985; Barrow 1993, 130–36). In the case of the park service, its centralized management, resources, and professionalism have been historically deployed to convert the national parks into a profit generating system of tourist centers.

MANAGEMENT OF THE NATIONAL PARK SYSTEM
PRIOR TO THE PARK SERVICE

The U.S. National Park Service was established in 1916 as a bureau of the Interior Department. It was created to centralize national park management. Prior to the establishment of the service, each national park and national monument was administratively separate and semiautonomous under the general authority of the Interior Department.[1] This lack of central management for the national park system created several difficulties in the areas of park services, park management, and park development. Historian Robert Shankland (1970) describes succinctly these problems and how they pertained to specific parks:

The concessioners operated widely variant regulations from park to park. The division of authority among the parks, and even inside a single park, came close to chaos. In Yellowstone all improvements and their appropriations were managed by an officer of the Army Corps of Engineers, who answered to neither the Interior Department nor the park superintendent; the superintendent was himself an Army officer, appointed by the Secretary of War; and "exclusive control" rested with the Secretary of the Interior. Crater Lake and Mount Rainier, like Yellowstone, used Army engineers for road-building and improvements, but in those two parks the superintendent was civilian, appointed by the Secretary of the Interior. On the other hand, Yosemite, Sequoia, and General Grant had Army superintendents but no Army engineers. (104)

Furthermore, without any single authority responsible for the park system, no one was directly responsible for assuring that the parks created were of sufficient quality to warrant national park status. Thus, the creation of parks was often the result of "pork barrel" politics. National park historian John Ise (1961, 186) argues that Mackinac, Platt, and Sullys Hill National Parks, created prior to the existence of the National Park Service, were the result of pressure politics and did not warrant park status. In addition to potentially degrading the park system through the creation of inferior parks, the addition of low-quality parks creates more parks among which a limited pool of resources must be divided (Ise 1961, 186).

THE CREATION OF THE NATIONAL PARK SERVICE

The first director of the National Park Service was Stephen T. Mather. Mather was a millionaire industrialist who made his fortune in the mining and processing of borax (Shankland 1970, chap. 3). He came to the Interior Department in 1915 as part of an effort to centralize the administration of the national park system. In 1911, and again in 1912, National Park Conferences were held. Both conferences called for the centralized management of the national parks. Railroad and automobile industry representatives, local business representatives, and others interested in the national parks attended these conferences (U.S. Department of the Interior 1912, 1–2; Ise 1961, 187–88; Sellars 1997, 32). The railroads represented at the 1911 conference, for example, were the Oregon Short Line, the Northern Pacific Railway, the Southern Pacific, the Atchison, Topeka & Santa Fe Railway System, and the Great Northern Railway (U.S. Department of the Interior 1912, 1–2).

The business community's support for the centralized management of the park system was predicated on the fact that the success of tourist-related "investment depended in part on the preservation of scenery through prevention of haphazard tourism development and other invasive commercial uses such as mining and lumbering" within the parks (Sellars 1997, 10). During the late nineteenth and early twentieth centuries, railroad firms, in particular, invested substantial amounts of capital to develop transportation services to the national parks and to develop park accommodations. The Northern Pacific, for example, built a railroad extension to Yellowstone. The Southern Pacific developed transportation services to the Yosemite, Sequoia, and General Grant national parks. Also, the Santa Fe Railroad built a railroad to the rim of the Grand Canyon (Runte 1974, 14–15). Examples of railroad investments into the area of park accommodations included the Northern Pacific in Yellowstone, the Great Northern in Glacier, the Union Pacific in Zion, Bryce and the Grand Canyon, and the Milwaukee & St. Paul in Mount Rainer (Shankland 1970, 134).

By 1911, the management of the national park system became centralized. In 1911, all park affairs were placed under the authority of W. B. Acker, an assistant attorney in the Interior Department, but he could only devote part of his time to park issues (Shankland 1970, 53). In 1913, the secretary of the interior assigned the national parks, among other duties, to the assistant to the secretary, the highest-level assignment the parks had received to that point. Among the assistant's other duties, however, were to manage the territories of Alaska and Hawaii, the Bureau of Education, and the federal buildings in the District of Columbia. The assistant secretary, Adolph C. Miller, was soon appointed to the Federal Reserve Board, which created the opening for Mather (Ise 1961, 187; Shankland 1970, 53–54). Unlike Miller, however, Mather's primary responsibility as assistant secretary was the national park system (Shankland 1970, chap. 6; Albright and Schenck 1999, 35–36).[2]

Stephen Mather, at the time of his appointment as assistant secretary, was a prominent member of organizations concerned with national park policy. As Mather's biographer, Robert Shankland (1970) explains Mather "was a member—which meant an active member—of the Sierra Club of California, the Prairie Club of Chicago, and the American Civic Association" (9). The American Civic Association and its president, J. Horace McFarland, were among the earliest proponents of the creation of a single professional government organization to manage the national parks. In addition, the American Civic Association was a strong and early proponent of utilizing the national parks as tourist attractions (U.S. Department of the Interior 1912, 17–19; Morrison 1995, chap. 11; Runte 1997, chap. 5; Young 1996, 465 and 468; Sellars 1997, 30 and 33–34).

Both the American Civic Association and the Sierra Club were part of an economic elite-led policy-planning network centered on public parks. In addition to Mather, these organizations had substantial connections to the business community. Terence Young, a historian of the American Civic Association, points out that throughout the association's history, its board of directors contained bankers and philanthropists (1996, 461; Morrison 1995, chap 6). Among them were George Foster Peabody, a New York banker and philanthropist, and Chicago businessman Franklin MacVeagh, both of whom were board members at the organization's founding (Morrison 1995, 94–95). In addition, John D. Rockefeller, Jr., was a longtime financial supporter of the American Civic Association (Albright, 26 March 1941; Ernst 1991d, 89 and 200). Furthermore, J. Horace McFarland himself was a wealthy printer from Harrisburg, Pennsylvania (Morrison 1995, chap. 3).

Given the composition of its membership, the Sierra Club, in particular, throughout most of its history has manifested the characteristics of a policy discussion group for members of the economic elite. Susan R. Schrepfer (1983) in her survey of the Sierra Club's early charter members found that approximately one-third were academics, and "the rest of them were almost all businessmen and lawyers working in San Francisco's financial district" (10). The club was founded in 1892. Schrepfer goes on to explain that business-people continued to compose a substantial portion of the club's membership and leadership until the 1960s (171–73). One of the most important connections between the early Sierra Club and the California business community was officials from the Southern Pacific Railroad (Orsi 1985). Among the club's charter members there were five from the politically and economically powerful railroad (Jones 1965, 37; Lamare 1994, 11–12; Pincetl 1999). This included the Southern Pacific's first vice president, C. H. Crocker, and its general ticket agent, T. H. Goodman (Jones 1965, 58). Mather's active membership in organizations such as the Sierra Club and the American Civic Association, as well as in other groups that were focused on parks, indicates that he served as a leader of this policy-planning network and as a conduit to achieving a political consensus among the network's economic elite membership, as well as among the economic elite in general on the issue of the national parks (Domhoff 1978, 1998; Barrow 1993, chap. 1).

While Mather was very interested in wilderness and its preservation, he was not an "expert" in any meaningful sense. He did not posses any degree in the areas of biology or wildlife management. Instead, his interest and knowledge of wilderness reflected that of a dilettante. His biographer explains that "Mather was not in the ecological know. His love for the birds and beasts was deep and genuine, but it was not erudite. He was more conversant with the trees and flowers, yet even in the presence of botany he showed greater feeling than knowledge" (Shankland 1970, 273).

The National Park Service came into existence the year after Mather came to the Interior Department. One of Mather's objectives when he joined the department was the creation of a bureau of national parks (Shankland 1970, 56; Albright and Cahn 1985, 32). The enabling legislation that created the park service, later entitled the Park Service Act, was written with the help of Mather and members of the American Civic Association (Shankland 1970, 101; Sellars 1997, chap. 2). National park historian Alfred Runte points out that the railroads lobbied on behalf of the legislation by sending prominent officials to testify before Congress (1997, 100).

THE PROFESSIONALIZATION OF THE
PARK SERVICE BUREAUCRACY

Stephen Mather was director of the National Park Service from its organization in 1917 until his health forced him to resign in 1928. During his tenure as director, Mather molded the park service into a professional organization. Prior to the existence of the service, appointments within the park system were part of the political spoils system. In a 1920 report, however, Mather wrote, "Nearly six years ago, I accepted the Department's invitation to undertake in the public interest the development of the national parks into a smoothly running, well-coordinated system" (as quoted in Shankland 1970, 243). By the early 1920s, Mather had succeeded in establishing a professionalized and well-managed service. Shankland (1970) points out that by late 1923 "most of the jitney politicians had been purged; Mather had filled the key superintendencies with young, intelligent, and eager administrators; the Washington office was humming; and three special field divisions (two of them unique in federal structure) had been organized and were at work" (252).

Mather was able to create a professionalized and capable park service staff in a relatively short period of time, because, in part, he resisted the extension of civil service privileges to service employees. Shankland (1970) explains that Mather denied civil service protection to park service employees until late in his tenure because Mather "felt that he had to be free to unload misfits and to shift his other men around until he had arrived at his best combination" (249). Park service rangers were made civil service employees in 1925. Park superintendents and custodians were made part of the civil service in 1931, after Mather retired (Shankland 1970, 249).

How did Mather build a professional organization in the park service without protecting its employees under civil service laws? In other words, why was the park service immune from patronage politics during Mather's state-building endeavor? The answer can be found with those individuals outside government who supported Mather, the park service, and the national parks. High-level members of the business community, in particular, played a prominent role in the effort to protect the service.

The greatest threat to Mather's bureaucratic organization came in 1921. When the Harding administration replaced the Wilson administration, Albert Fall was appointed as secretary of interior. Fall was widely considered "a hack politician from deep in the land-grab belt" (Shankland 1970, 217). Mather knew that nothing prevented Fall from firing him and the capable personnel that he had recruited into the service. Shankland (1970) describes how, given Fall's political background, Mather felt that his efforts over the last several years to build an efficient and effective park service were under a mortal threat:

Mather could sense manifold calamities. This would be the first change of administration in the Park Service's short experience; the superintendents and rangers
were non-civil-service, and there was no precedent at all against Fall's firing the
whole roster, and Mather with them, and taking on a gang of tinhorns. Not only
was there no precedent against it; there was nothing in Fall's record of public service to point to anything else. (217)

Additionally, Mather also believed the national park system was not safe
with Fall as interior secretary. Not only did Mather see the park service threatened gravely by Fall's appointment, but, given Fall's background, he also
believed the park system itself was in great danger. Shankland (1970) again
describes Mather's perception of Fall, and his attendant fears:

Fall seemed sure to favor the loosest kind of protectorate. Though unequivocally
a politician first, he mixed also in mining, stock-raising, and ranching, and was
known to view those pursuits as among man's loftiest. In mien and manner he was
a pulp-fiction Westerner, an hombre who put on no airs except that one. Thinking about him, Mather could hear the crash of falling trees and the sound of dis-
tant dam construction. (217)

To protect the park service and the park system, friends of the service, and
of Mather's, rallied to protect both. In one case, a *Los Angeles Times* reporter
warned Fall, in Mather's presence, that his newspaper and its owner and publisher, Harry Chandler, "were particularly interested in Mather" (as quoted in
Shankland 1970, 217–18). This warning came the day of Harding's inauguration. In the summer of 1921 Mather and Fall jointly toured some of the
national parks in the far West, and "at Yosemite, the Yosemite National Park
Company gave a large dinner in [Fall and Mather's] honor, and one by one
Mather's *illustrious* California friends rose and extolled him and his park tri-
umphs" [emphasis added] (Shankland 1970, 218–19). Historian Donald Swain
(1970) explains that when Fall and Mather's tour arrived "in southern California, Harry Chandler, publisher of the *Los Angeles Times*, and other successful businessmen extolled the virtues of the National Park Service. In San Francisco and Seattle the same thing happened, as park enthusiasts and Mather's
friends rallied unanimously behind him" (144). Fall promised Mather that he
would not interfere with park service policy or personnel, and he never did
(Shankland 1970, 218).

Fall's policy of noninterference toward the park service was not the result
of some change of attitude by Fall toward the nation's resources and the
national parks. On their trip West, after he promised not to interfere with the
park service, Fall expressed unabashedly to Mather and Mather's assistant,
Horace Albright, his utilitarian attitude toward the nation's resources. Fall
held that the U.S. government should not restrict, in any way, the use of nat-

ural resources. Without reservation Fall pronounced that "I stand for opening up every resource" (as quoted in Shankland 1970, 220). When discussing
Albert Fall's attitude toward natural resources as secretary of the interior, one
has to invoke his duplicitous conduct in the Teapot Dome Scandal, where as
a result of his role in pilfering the U.S. oil reserves, Fall spent time in prison.

Nor during his short tenure as secretary of the interior (1921–1923) did Fall
view the national park system as a sacred cow. In 1922, Fall, with the aid of
local chambers of commerce, attempted to force into the national park system
a site of inferior quality located in southwestern New Mexico (Shankland
1970, 221–22; Albright and Cahn 1985, 129–35). The proposed park was a
clear instance of pork barrel politics. In describing the quality of, and Mather's
attitude toward, the secretary's proposed park, Shankland (1970) explains that
"Mather wanted no part of bringing this scandalous freak into the national-
park system" (222). Furthermore, in addition to Fall's proposed park being of
extremely poor quality, the park's enabling legislation, written by Fall and the
chambers of commerce, would have allowed hunting, grazing, timber harvesting, and mining, as well as other forms of resource development in the
park (Shankland 1970, 222; Albright and Cahn 1985, 130). Therefore, the
park, if admitted under Fall's legislation, would have grossly violated the park
service's policy of prohibiting hunting and resource extraction in the national
parks. The proposed park did not enter the system.

The Leadership of the National Park Service

Throughout most of the park service's history the directorship has been not a
civil service position. This means that directors can be summarily dismissed and
replaced without regard to professional credentials. Despite this lack of legal
protection, the park service throughout most of its history has avoided politically motivated appointments. Until 1972 the park service had only had seven
directors, including Mather. With the exclusion of one, Mather's first six successors came up within the service. These directors ostensibly received their
appointments on the basis of purely professional criteria (Everhart 1983, 150).
The sixth, Newton Drury, who served as service director from 1940 to 1951,
was a highly respected preservationist from the Save-the-Redwoods League.

The park service leadership avoided political appointments during the first
fifty-six years of its existence because of the individuals outside government who
historically supported the service. It has already been described how the park
service was protected from political appointments in 1921. In 1953, when the
Eisenhower administration replaced the Truman administration, the new secretary of the interior, Douglas McKay, asked the Civil Service Commission to
withdraw the top six positions within the park service from the civil service. The
commission followed suit. The service positions divested of civil service protection were the director, the director's secretary, the chief counsel, and the three

assistant directors (Shankland 1970, 312). In response to this threat to the park service leadership, John D. Rockefeller, Jr. (JDR Jr.), a longtime supporter and contributor to the national park system (Ernst 1991c), intervened personally to protect the service. Rockefeller, routed through his son, who was then under-secretary of health, education, and welfare, a letter to the Interior Department. The letter, addressed to his son, Nelson A. Rockefeller, expressed:

> A word at your [Nelson's] convenience would be appreciated. It would appear that Mr. [Horace] Albright thinks this action that has been taken will react unfavor-ably on the Park Service which he has done so much to build up and which I have always regarded as one of the best manned and operated of any of the government departments of which I know.[3] (21 August 1953)

In response to JDR Jr.'s letter, Secretary McKay responded personally with a letter of his own. In it he explains to Rockefeller that "I assure you that in the foreseeable future there is no intention of exercising the authority to remove any of the officials in the affected positions" (McKay, 2 September 1953). Immediately after receiving McKay's letter, Rockefeller responded directly to the secretary. Here JDR Jr. accepts McKay's assurances regarding the leader-ship of the park service. He goes on to explain to McKay that "I have always counted it a privilege to do what I could to further the wise and farseeing pur-poses of that [the Park] Service" (Rockefeller, 5 September 1953).

According to historian Robin Winks (1997), the importance of profession-alism to the park service "was a message JDR Jr. would repeat often" (80). In addition to his actions in 1953, in 1920 JDR Jr. lobbied President-elect Hard-ing to protect the service from political appointments (Foresta 1984, 22–23). JDR Jr.'s son, Laurence (LSR), also took an active role on park service issues (Winks 1997, chap. 6). Laurence Rockefeller's biographer explains that "LSR helped prevent [Park Service Director] Wirth's possible dismissal in 1953 and 1961" (Winks 1997, 114).[4]

The park service leadership was also able to avoid politically motivated appointments in the 1968 partisan exchange of presidential administrations. Upon assuming office in 1969, the new secretary of the interior fired all bureau chiefs, except that of the service's (Everhart 1983, 151). At the beginning of Nixon's second term, however, then–park service director, George Hartzog, was fired by the president's direct order. His dismissal was ostensibly predicated on an incident that Hartzog had earlier with Nixon's close friend Bebe Rebozo (Hartzog 1988, 233–38, and 241). Hartzog was replaced by a Nixon political operative, Ronald Walker. Following Hartzog, the park service had five direc-tors in eight years, many of whom were chosen for political reasons (Everhart 1983, 150–55; Sellars 1997, 232–33).[5] The service's turmoil coincided with the radicalization of environmental politics during the late 1960s and early 1970s. Specifically, during this period of time many self-proclaimed and recently mobilized environmentalists strongly criticized corporate America for its treatment of the environment. This putative radicalization alienated more conservative supporters of environmental issues.[6] Park service historian Ronald Foresta (1984) observes that "the 1960s and, to a greater extent, the 1970s, saw the agency lose much of the active support of the nation's business and professional elite, support present at the founding of the Service and carefully nurtured by its directors from Mather through Hartzog" (71).

The park service's ties to the economic elite have been reflected historically in the membership of the Advisory Board on National Parks, Historic Sites, Buildings, and Monuments (Foresta 1984, 71). Later the board's name was changed to the National Park System Advisory Board. Historian Robin Winks (1997) describes the role of this board and its membership in the following:

> This board, which was established in the 1930s, provided a forum of knowledge-able and well-placed individuals who could buffer the National Park Service from political interference. Members were appointed for indefinite terms, they took their charge seriously and saw themselves as stewards who helped to protect the director of the Park Service from undue pressure by commercial and local interests who promoted unworthy park proposals, and the members often had substantial private means or the capacity to broker private funds to support park projects. (81)

Winks goes on to point out that "JDR Jr. was never a member of the [National Park System Advisory] board, but there almost always was a representative from JDR Jr., and later from Laurance Rockefeller, in the group." As Winks explains, however, "Unhappily this working relationship began to erode in the 1970s" (81).

In 1980, however, with the consultation and consent of senior park service administrators, Russ Dickenson was appointed director. Dickenson survived the change of administrations in 1981 (Everhart 1983, 154–55). Reagan's secretary of the interior, James Watt, replaced all bureau heads, except that of the service's (Everhart 1983, 29). This professionally motivated appointment coincided with a return to normalcy in the political climate of environmental politics.

THE PARK SERVICE'S RELATIONSHIP WITH THE NATIONAL PARK ISSUE NETWORK

During Mather's tenure as service director (1917–1928), a clear division developed within the national park issue network. Two philosophically distinct groups developed. One, the "pure" preservationists, valued the national parks and the wilderness within them for their intrinsic value. The other, the "use" preservationists, composed mostly of business firms and their representatives, valued the national parks for the income they generated. As a result of these different conceptions of the national parks and wilderness, a tension developed between these network members. On the one hand, use preservationists wanted the national parks developed so they could accommodate tourists and their motor vehicles. On the other hand, the pure preservationists wanted the national parks to be left as close to their pristine state as possible. Later, beginning in the late 1960s, many pure preservationists wanted the parks to be venues where ecosystems could operate in an unfettered manner (Frome 1992; Sellars 1997, chaps. 6 and 7; Sellers 1999).

Mather came from that portion of the national park issue network that favored and promoted the use of the parks. One of Mather's primary objectives when assuming leadership of the park system was to interest the public in the parks and to develop the parks so they could accommodate tourists. Shortly after being appointed assistant secretary, Mather published an article dated 6 March 1915 in *The American Review of Reviews*, entitled "The National Parks on a Business Basis." Here he wrote that "the Government must do its part to make the national parks as cheap and as attractive as possible to the people" (430). Mather went on to assert that "our national parks are practically lying fallow, and only await proper *development* to bring them into their own" [emphasis added] (430). Shankland (1970) explains that upon coming to the Interior Department Mather sought to "get the public excited over the national parks; make park travel easier, by promoting wholesale improvements in hotels, camps, and other concessions and in roads and other transportation facilities both inside the national parks and outside" (156). Additionally, using his own resources and those of the park service, Mather encouraged tourism to the national parks through an aggressive publicity campaign (Shankland 1970, chap. 8). He pursued this pro-tourism and pro-development course throughout his tenure as service director (Shankland 1970, chaps. 8, 10–12; Sellars 1997, chap. 3).

Mather wrote, or helped write, what is considered the "Magna Carta" of the National Park Service, which established the core policy principles of the park service (Shankland 1970, 345; Sellars 1997, 245; Albright and Schenck 1999, chap. 21). This document came formally in a letter from Secretary of Interior Franklin K. Lane to Mather, but as Ise (1961) points out it was "doubtless written in co-operation with Mather, or more likely written by Mather" (195; Wirth 1980, 40).[7] This letter outlined administrative policy for the national park system and continues to guide the park service on policy matters. In referring to Lane's letter, Shankland (1970) explains that "it has become customary for each incoming Secretary of the Interior to reaffirm these principles in a policy letter addressed to the Director of the Service" (345). Swain (1970) points out that "announced officially in the form of a letter from Lane to Mather, dated May 13, 1918, these policy objectives have remained the core of national park administration ever since" (89). Park service historian Richard Sellars (1997) explains that the "Lane Letter of 1918 was fundamental dogma for decades, and deemed official policy as late as the 1970s" (286).

This letter mandated the usage of the national parks as tourist centers. It specified, for example, that "every opportunity should be afforded the public, wherever possible, to enjoy the national parks" (Lane, 13 May 1918). The letter goes on to stipulate that "automobiles and motorcycles will be permitted in all of the national parks; in fact, the parks will be kept accessible by any means practicable." One of the most significant precepts established in Lane's letter prescribed that the park service closely cooperate with economic actors to promote the national parks as tourist centers. This precept specifically mandated that Mather, as park service director:

> utilize to the fullest extent the opportunity afforded by the Railroad Administration in appointing a committee of western railroads to inform the traveling public how to comfortably reach the national parks; you should diligently extend and use the splendid cooperation developed during the last three years among chambers of commerce, tourist bureaus, and automobile highway associations, for the purpose of spreading information about our national parks and facilitating their use and enjoyment. (Lane, 13 May 1918) [At the time this letter was written, the railroads were formally managed by the Railroad Administration.]

Mather's use and development policies were continued by his successors (Nash 1982, chap. 15; Sellars 1997).[8] Under both the Albright (1929–1933) and Cammerer (1933–1940) administrations, road building in the national parks expanded substantially as the service's budget grew to new levels (Ise 1961, 326–27, and 362; Swain 1970, 189; Sellars 1997, chap. 4). Also, to offset the effects of the Depression "in 1934 the Park Service put on a big travel promotion campaign through the co-operation of concessioners, railroads and other transportation agencies, automobile associations, oil companies, chambers of commerce, and civic associations" (Ise 1961, 356). Due in large part to World War II, there was a lull in the park service's development activities under Drury's administration (1940–1951) (Ise 1961, 447–48; Sellars 1997, chap. 5).

In 1956, however, the park service undertook an aggressive and long-term campaign to develop the park system. As part of this campaign, a plan entitled "Mission 66" was put forth. It mapped out park system development over a ten-year period. Under Mission 66 the park service updated and expanded park system services and infrastructure. Ultimately, under this plan approximately $1 billion was expended on tourist-related development within the park system (Ise 1961, 546–50; Wirth 1980, chap. 9; Worsnop 1993, 469; Sellars 1997, 173–91; Barringer 1999). The park service continues to prioritize making the national parks tourist-friendly (Frome 1992; Worsnop 1993; Sellars 1997, chap. 7; Janofsky, 25 July 1999; Nieves and Wald, 28 March 2000). Given the service's historic policy of developing the national parks and managing them for the purposes of tourism, its budgetary expenditures and bureaucratic development are in substantial part subsidies to the firms that profit monetarily from the parks (Rothman 1998, 1999).[9]

The Pure Preservationists and the National Park Service

As the park service continued its pro-tourism policy under Mather as well as under subsequent service directors, it alienated a significant number of the pure preservationist faction of the national park issue network.[10] Beginning in the 1920s and 1930s, pure preservationists criticized the service for its emphasis on promoting tourism and development in the national parks. In 1922, for example, Emerson Hough, a "big name writer and self-styled nature lover," reproved the Yellowstone superintendent, and the park service, for increasing tourism to the park and expanding the use of the automobile in Yellowstone (Swain 1970, 48 and 139). Also, "in the late 1920s and 1930s [Horace] Albright's pragmatic views [as service director] came under attack from avid wilderness disciples, such as Robert Sterling Yard, of the National Parks Association, and to a lesser extent, Robert Marshall, founder of the Wilderness Society" (320). Swain further explains:

> As the 1920s progressed an increasing number of conservation purists, especially in the Sierra Club and the Seattle Mountaineers, organizations dedicated to the preservation of wilderness areas, questioned the wisdom of packing the parks with visitors and allowing automobiles to "ruin" the natural atmosphere. (139)

Susan R. Schrepfer, the historian of the Save-the-Redwoods League, describes how as early as the 1920s members within the league felt that the park service's development policies were despoiling the national parks. She explains that members within the league "had soon begun to feel that the National Park Service was degrading the inspirational value of national parks and destroying their primitive character" (1983, 52). Ise (1961) reports that "since the early thirties the Park Service has been subject to some criticism from a growing number of 'purists' and wilderness lovers, who . . . want [the national parks] kept more largely as wilderness areas, with few roads or none at all" (647). In 1992, Michael Frome, a longtime and leading pure preservationist, complained that under the stewardship of the park service, "Americans are loving the [national] parks to death. Too many automobiles cause congestion and pollution. Low-flying airplanes and helicopters pollute the wilderness with noise. . . . Toxic chemicals ruin the air and water" (4).

At one point, many pure preservationists came to view the U.S. Forest Service as a better protector of wilderness than the National Park Service. Beginning in the 1920s, with demand for its timber low, the forest service, under an administrative policy, set aside tracts of forest as "wilderness" or "primitive" areas within the national forests. Commercial activities were either curtailed sharply, or altogether prohibited, from these tracts (Robbins 1982; Cohen 1988, 111; Hirt 1994, xxv). With this policy, the forest service came to be viewed by many of the pure preservationists as a champion of wilderness. In the 1930s, for example, the Wilderness Society and the National Parks Association opposed the creation of Kings Canyon National Park out of a wilderness area that was managed by the forest service (Schrepfer 1983, 61; Dilsaver and Tweed 1990, 210; Sellars 1997, 143).

The view of the forest service as the guardian of primitive wilderness ended in the post–World War II period. With the timber industry increasing its demand for timber within the national forests, the forest service began to abandon its wilderness policies. As a result, timber production was initiated in areas designated formerly as protected wilderness (Frome 1974, chap. 9; Cohen 1988, 187–211; Hirt 1994, xxv, 225–28). It was disappointment and dissatisfaction among the pure preservationists, with both the park service and forest service, that led to their initiation and strong support for the Wilderness Act of 1964 (Frome 1974, chap. 9; Cohen 1988, chap. 5; Hirt 1994, 229 and chap. 10; Sellars 1997, 191–94). Under this act, portions within the public domain are permanently designated as "wilderness." Resource exploitation, road building, and the erection of permanent structures are restricted in wilderness areas (Allin 1982).

CONCLUSION

The creation and development of the National Park Service are consistent with the economic elite model of policymaking. A member of the economic elite, millionaire industrialist Stephen Mather was the park service's most influential director. Mather was a leader of the policy-planning network that dealt with national park policies. He was specifically active in an organization that promoted the centralized and professional management of the parks and their use as tourist attractions (i.e., the American Civic Association). The park service was developed by Mather into an institution that promoted and subsidized tourism, and as a result it served the economic needs of the corporate community. Therefore, as the railroad industry, and other economic sectors, began to expand their investments in a transportation and accommodation infrastructure in the national parks during the early twentieth century, the park service was created and it channeled public monies into attracting tourists to the parks and managing the parks to maximize tourist attendance.

Additionally, members of the economic elite outside of government were also active in the creation, development, and maintenance of the service. Railroad firms, as well as other economic interests, through the national park conferences called for the centralization of national park management. Railroad representatives also lobbied Congress for the creation of the park service. Furthermore, it was found that the service's professional bureaucracy and its pro-tourism leadership were historically protected through, in large part, the efforts of economic elites.

Despite the well-developed issue network that surrounded national park policies, these policies were not substantial compromises between network members. The service's pro-tourism policies alienated the pure preservationists and prompted them to seek out another government bureaucracy—the forest service and, ultimately, new wilderness legislation to satisfy its policy preferences.

In conclusion, the National Park Service's history demonstrates how an ostensibly professional and politically insulated bureaucracy can be developed to the benefit of a specific interest group. The bureaucratic norms and principles on which the service is built are designed to serve the interests of tourist-related industries. Within the park service professionalism is largely equated with the managed exploitation of wilderness as a tourist attraction. Sellars (1997), a historian with the park service, explains that the service's "overriding emphasis on tourism development [has historically] fostered the ascendancy of certain professions [within it] such as landscape architecture and engineering, and largely determined the Service's . . . perception of what is right and proper for the parks" (4). In contrast, Sellars's (1997) extensive history of the park service and its management of the national parks demonstrates that within the service, ecologically centered values and views have been and continue to be politically and bureaucratically peripheral. Thus, contrary to the claims of state autonomy theorists (Skowronek 1982; Skocpol 1985; Klyza 1992), the history of the service shows that professionalization and bureaucratic development do not necessarily enhance the ability of state agencies to behave autonomously.

NOTES

1. Some monuments were administered by the Department of Agriculture, and two were housed in the War Department along with military national parks (Ise 1961, 185).

2. When Mather came to the Interior Department, there were thirteen national parks and eighteen national monuments under the jurisdiction of the Interior Department (Shankland 1970, 56).

3. Horace Albright and John D. Rockefeller, Jr. were longtime friends and often collaborated on national park matters (Ernst 1991c).

4. For a discussion of how the Rockefellers favored the use of the national parks, see Winks (1997, chap. 5).

5. Sellars (1997) explains that with the fluctuations that occurred in the service leadership during the 1970s, "the regional directors assumed greater control" of park service policies (233).

6. One example of those alienated is Laurence Rockefeller, who has historically been active on wilderness and other conservation issues (Collier and Horowitz 1976, 388–404; Winks 1997). Rockefeller family biographers, Collier and Horowitz (1976), explain:

After Earth Day, 1970, brought ecology to the foreground of the public conscience and stimulated the growth of environmental action groups all across the country, Laurence's [Rockefeller] dilemma became clear. He may have privately abhorred the oil spills that blackened the beaches of Santa Barbara and San Francisco, but he could not publicly align himself with people picketing the oil companies and making antibusiness statements. (401)

7. In his posthumously published autobiography, Albright takes sole credit for composing Lane's letter (Albright and Schenck 1999, chap. 21). He acknowledges, however, that he wrote the letter to conform to Mather's "spirit" and "ideas" (Albright and Schenck 1999, 275). He also explains that "when Mather did get [the letter], he never criticized a word, just congratulated me on the effort" (Albright and Schenck 1999, 275).

8. Within the national park system are parks labeled "wilderness" parks. Included among these parks are Acadia, Great Smoky, Grand Teton, Isle Royale, and the Everglades (Ise 1961, 370). Wilderness parks tend to be relatively less developed than other parks, such as Yellowstone and Yosemite. There is no park service policy, however, that distinguishes a wilderness park from other conventional parks. Therefore, some wilderness parks, for example, have accommodations and roads, and others only have roads (Ise 1961, 370). Ise argues that wilderness parks are relatively undeveloped not because of any departure from the development policies of the park service, "but because conditions in the areas suggested that as the most appropriate policy" (370). Subsequently, as circumstances change so can the park service's policy in specific wilderness parks. Thus, in September 1965, the National Park Service proposed "a major, multimillion-dollar transmountain route across the Smokies wilderness into Tennessee" (Frome 1974, 180).

9. The National Park Service currently spends approximately $2 billion annually in its management of the national parks and monuments.

10. For a pure preservationist critique of park service development policies, see Frome (1974, chap. 6; 1992).

4

~

Wilderness Preservation Policy
The Cases of Yosemite Park and Jackson Hole

In this chapter, and in the succeeding one, I examine three instances of public policymaking. All three involve wilderness preservation issues. These case studies are (1) the California State government's recession of Yosemite National Park to the federal government, (2) the incorporation of the Jackson Hole area into the national park system, and (3) the creation of Redwood National Park. All three case studies suggest that, in the case of achieving wilderness preservation policy goals, active economic elite political support is a necessary condition. Additionally, the first and third case studies suggest that wealthy donors and wealthy board members, in the case of environmental groups, are not passive actors in the process of formulating policy goals and political discourses.

THE SIERRA CLUB

In 1892 the Sierra Club was formed to protect Yosemite park and to help its members enjoy the Sierra Nevada mountains. It was composed of both intellectuals and members from the San Francisco business community. Holway Jones (1965), in his history of the early Sierra Club, describes the leading role that California business members played in the formation of the organization, as well as the role that its business members played in the club's political battles. He specifically outlines the controversy over the withdrawal of Yosemite Park from the state government of California.

The Creation of the Sierra Club

Following the example of wilderness clubs established in the East, the idea to establish a wilderness (or mountain) club in the San Francisco area began to circulate among the faculty of the University of California in the 1880s (Jones 1965, 7–8). John Muir, whose writings had done a great deal to popularize the Yosemite area, had many friends among the university's faculty and joined this effort to establish a wilderness club. In 1891, through the influence of Robert Underwood Johnson, associate editor of *Century Magazine*, the idea of a wilderness club developed into a "defense association" (Jones 1965, 8). This organization, which eventually became the Sierra Club, would be designed to both help members enjoy California parks as well as to protect them politically (Jones 1965, 8–9).

It was several months, however, before formal steps were taken to form the Sierra Club. It was not until Warren Olney, a leading San Francisco attorney, agreed to help in the formation of the club that it was established. After Olney agreed to participate in the founding of the club, Muir, who himself married into a wealthy family (Jones 1965, 8; Orsi 1985, 137–38), wrote to one of his faculty friends that "I am greatly interested in the formation of an Alpine Club. I think with you and Mr. Olney that the time has come when such a club should be organized" (as quoted in Jones 1965, 9). Olney, who prepared the Sierra Club's Articles of Incorporation, was elected first vice president of the club and to its board of directors by the club's members (Jones 1965, 9). Muir was elected the club's president. The three other club officers were academics. Jones (1965) describes in the following what each of these officers brought to the Sierra Club:

> It was fortunate . . . that men like Senger, Armes, and Branner, who had strong academic ties and were able to interest students and colleagues, and Olney, who supplied the necessary legal advice and had a wide acquaintance among lawyers, and business people throughout the Bay Area, were also fervent believers in the Club and readily joined their talents with Muir's. (10)

Overall, as described in the preceding chapter, the club had strong ties to the business community. Also noted in chapter 3, among the most important connections between the early Sierra Club and the California business community included officials from the economically and politically powerful Southern Pacific Railroad (Mowry 1951, chap. 1; Jones 1965, 37; Orsi 1985; Lamare 1994, 11–12; Pincetl 1999). The interest that the Southern Pacific Railroad took in the Sierra Club and in the Yosemite park is not surprising considering the railroad profited significantly from the tourist travel generated by the park (Jones 1965, 47; Orsi 1985, 144). Jones argues that the Southern Pacific proved instrumental in expanding the Yosemite park in 1890, maintaining the new park land under federal control, and in determining the contours of the expansion. These changes were made despite the fact that the state commission governing the state park publicly opposed federal control of any of the park's land (1965, 43–47).

Recession of Yosemite National Park

In June 1864, the federal government gave the state of California the land encompassing the Yosemite Valley and the adjoining Mariposa Big Trees for the exclusive purpose of establishing a state park. In 1905, the Yosemite park was receded to the national government. The issue of recession to the federal government created a division between the business members and intellectuals of the Sierra Club, a division that immobilized the club on the issue of recession.

From the club's inception the issue of recession created discord within it. On one side stood Muir and on the other was Olney. As early as 1890, Muir complained to Robert Johnson of the state's management of the Yosemite Park. He specifically alleged that appointments to the state commission that managed the park were often political in nature and that as a result the park's management suffered (Jones 1965, 55). In addition to Johnson and Muir, Charles D. Robinson, an artist who spent considerable time in the valley (Jones 1965, 36), also advocated the park's recession to the federal government.

Critics of the state commission felt that it was ineffective in protecting the Yosemite Valley from activities that were destroying its wildlife and scenic amenities. A particular focus of their ire was the unauthorized grazing and logging that frequently occurred within the valley under the state commission's stewardship (Orsi 1985, 143). Also, around the park unsightly sheds, stables, and fences were erected (Runte 1997, 59). Furthermore, critics of the park's management complained about changes made to the park by individuals who sought to profit from tourism. In one particularly egregious occurrence, "one hotel keeper . . . actually cut a swath through the trees to provide his barroom with an unobstructed view of Yosemite Falls" (Runte 1997, 59).

In the early 1890s, an Interior Department report found that a large majority of the people residing around the valley were in support of transferring the park to the federal government. It had been decided, however, by the Interior Department that recession of the park would first require approval by the California state legislature (Jones 1965, 56).

Despite Muir's commitment to transferring the park to the federal government, he was unable to immediately persuade the club to support recession. As early as June 1892 Muir, Robinson, and William Armes, a faculty member at the University of California, a club director and officer, attempted unsuccessfully to solicit the club's support for recession (Jones 1965, 57). The club's silence on this issue stemmed in part from Olney's opposition (Jones 1965, 61). In light of the Sierra Club's unwillingness to fight for recession, Robinson, for one, believed that the club was under the control of its business members, and, in particular, the Southern Pacific Railroad (Jones 1965, 57–59). The Southern Pacific Railroad publicly opposed the recession of the park to the federal government and away from the state commission over which the railroad held considerable influence (Jones 1965, 67–68). It was not until 1897 that Olney supported recession, and, in 1905, when a bill for recession was before the California state legislature, the club lobbied strongly in favor of it (Jones 1965, 62, 64–65).

While the Sierra Club was finally able to openly support the recession of Yosemite Park, it was the support provided by the Southern Pacific Railroad that allowed the withdrawal of the park by the federal government (Orsi 1985, 149–50). Jones (1965) argues that the Southern Pacific sought to gain "advantage for itself through quiet support of recession while continuing to wield influence over [the] Board [managing Yosemite]" (68). William Colby, a leader of the Sierra Club, with the assistance of William H. Mills, head of the Southern Pacific Land Department, wrote the 1905 recession bill for presentation to the state legislature (Jones 1965, 67). Historian Richard J. Orsi (1985) points out that the owner of the Southern Pacific, E. H. Harriman, directed William F. Herrin, head of the railroad's legal department, "to mobilize the company's supporters in the [California] legislature behind retrocession" (150). Jones (1965) points out that the behind the scenes support provided by the Southern Pacific was pivotal to the passage of the recession bill:

> A comparison of the senators who finally voted "yes" with the names of those the [San Francisco] *Examiner* claimed as against recession nearly two months earlier shows that at least nine men changed their opinion in this interval. Herrin [the Southern Pacific's lobbyist] had planned his strategy well. Certain senators "who were notoriously controlled by the railroad company were loud in their opposition to recession," yet voted *for* Belshaw's bill [the recession legislation] in the showdown. This game of "divide and conquer" played by the Southern Pacific was cleverly designed to keep the public and the press from guessing the real position of the Railroad [author's emphasis]. (72–73)

The final vote in the state senate was twenty-one to thirteen in favor of recession (Jones 1965, 72). Muir specifically credited the Southern Pacific Railroad and E. H. Harriman for the passage of the recession bill in the California senate. Muir wrote to Johnson that "we might have failed to get the bill through the Senate but for the help of Mr. Harriman, though of course his name or his company were never in sight through all the fight" (as quoted in Orsi 1985, 150).

When Yosemite Park was withdrawn by the federal government, the Southern Pacific Railroad had the size of the park reduced to suit its business needs. To compete with a new railroad line, the Southern Pacific successfully eliminated more than ten thousand acres from the southwest corner of the park. The Yosemite Valley Railroad Company, a Southern Pacific competitor, had recently gained approval to build a railroad within the Merced River Canyon—

"the natural gateway to Yosemite Valley and the only route open all year" (Jones 1965, 74). The park reduction allowed the Southern Pacific to build a railroad line near the rim of the valley, thus allowing it to compete with the new Yosemite Valley line. This modification to the park's border was included in the federal legislation that withdrew the park from the state of California. The reduction was made to the park despite the opposition of the secretary of the interior, the superintendent of the park, and the chair of the federal Yosemite Park Commission, as well as a letter from the Sierra Club expressing opposition to the reduction (Jones 1965, 75–77).

JOHN D. ROCKEFELLER, JR. AND WILDERNESS PRESERVATION

I now shift my analysis to the preservation of the Jackson Hole area. Unlike the recession of Yosemite Park, where the Southern Pacific's political activity proved decisive, the incorporation of Jackson Hole into the national park system precipitated a political confrontation between two politically substantial factions of the business community—namely, the livestock industry and the Rockefeller family. As a result of this political face-off, the battle to preserve Jackson Hole stalemated for more than two decades.

Throughout much of his life John D. Rockefeller, Jr. (JDR Jr.) actively and generously contributed to parks throughout the country. Between 1924 and 1960, he contributed approximately $40 million to state and national parks (Ernst 1991b, 4).[1] Some of his most substantial gifts went toward the creation, expansion, and/or development of Acadia, the Great Smoky Mountains, Shenandoah, Yosemite, and Grand Teton National Parks. In addition, Rockefeller gave $2 million toward the expansion of the California state redwood parks (Ernst 1991b). His most important and significant contribution to the national park system was the Jackson Hole area.

Throughout the period of Rockefeller's munificence, he maintained a relationship with the National Park Service and many of the wilderness preservation groups. This relationship was maintained primarily through Horace Albright. The Rockefeller–Albright–Park Service–wilderness groups complex composed a policy-planning network that would influence wilderness policy throughout the middle portion of the twentieth century and is responsible for the incorporation of the Jackson Hole area into the national park system.

JDR Jr. and Horace Albright first met in 1924, while Albright was superintendent of Yellowstone National Park. Rockefeller, and his sons, were visiting Yellowstone during the summer. Soon after Rockefeller's trip to the national park he wrote Albright. In his letter, Rockefeller commented that many of Yellowstone's roads were marred by downed trees and other debris that were along the roadside. He then offered to contribute financially to the clearing of these roadsides (Rockefeller, 15 August 1924). Albright accepted Rockefeller's offer (2 September 1924). Over the next several years, Rockefeller contributed $49,430 for this road work (Ernst 1991b, 9). Throughout this project Albright and JDR Jr. corresponded. Albright, in particular, would write Rockefeller detailed reports on the project that included information on the progress of the roadside cleanup, how Rockefeller's money was being used, and what additional monies would be required (Ernst 1991d). This project served as the basis on which the park service began to clear roadsides regularly (Albright, 11 March 1930; Swain 1970, 155).

Through the success of the Yellowstone project, JDR Jr. became a close friend of Albright and the park service. Swain (1970), Albright's biographer, explains that Rockefeller's visit to Yellowstone "was the beginning of a cordial and remarkably productive friendship between Albright and Rockefeller" (154). Peter Collier and David Horowitz (1976), Rockefeller family biographers, explain that through JDR Jr., Albright became "part of the Rockefellers' so-called 'outer circle' " (149). From 1924 until JDR Jr.'s death in 1960, Albright and Rockefeller would regularly correspond and meet over park service matters (Ernst 1991d).

In Christmas 1926, and again when Albright became park service director in 1929, JDR Jr. gave Albright cash gifts (Albright, 4 January 1927 and 15 January 1929). While the sum of these gifts is unknown, the gift that Rockefeller gave Albright when the latter became service director was substantial enough to make a significant contribution toward Albright's efforts to obtain a house in suburban Washington, D.C. In expressing his gratitude to JDR Jr., Albright told him that "your gift, Mr. Rockefeller, is going to be of great aid to me in getting a home out on the edge of the city [Washington, D.C.]" (15 January 1929).

Joseph W. Ernst (1991b), a Rockefeller family archivist, explains that "until the 1950s, each change in [park service] directors brought a response from [John D.] Rockefeller [Jr.], usually a letter commenting on the man's activities and including a small [cash] gift" (18). Further, in 1939 JDR Jr. gave Assistant Park Service Secretary Arno Cammerer $1,000 after Cammerer suffered a heart attack (Rockefeller, 19 July 1939; Albright, 22 July 1939).[2] Cammerer would later serve as service director for eight months in 1951.

Horace Albright's Post–National Park Service Career

Albright resigned as park service director in August 1933 to assume the positions of vice president and general manager for the United States Potash Company. He would later become its president. This firm mined and marketed potash—primarily utilized as a fertilizer. Potash also has applications as gun powder. Despite his executive position, Albright remained active on national park and wilderness preservation issues until his death in 1987. As a result of his political activity both in the fertilizer industry and on wilderness matters, Albright became what Domhoff would label a member of the "power elite" that focused both of these issues. In other words, Albright was a political leader for the business community in the areas of potash and wilderness preservation.

Albright's political leadership on business issues, specifically fertilizer and potash, was manifested by his appointment to various advisory committees during World War II. These committees were formed during the war and were part of the big business and government alliance developed under the exigencies of the war. Under this arrangement, business executives, through various boards and committees, were entrusted with the regulation and management of the U.S. economy during the war. During their government service, these executives would continue to draw their salaries from their companies and only receive a dollar a year in compensation from the U.S. government. Hence, Albright became what was known as a "dollar-a-year" man (Swain 1970).

Albright assumed an even more prominent position on National Park Service matters. Swain (1970) explains that "when Albright left the Park Service he vowed that he would keep in touch with the bureau's affairs and make himself available as an informal consultant and lobbyist in behalf of the national parks. Over the years, he more than made good his promises" (244). Swain goes on to point out that Albright's "loyalty and devotion to the National Park Service never flagged. He kept himself well informed about the bureau's problems. On his frequent trips to Washington he lobbied tirelessly for national park causes" (245). Albright maintained a close and consultative relationship with service directors and the secretaries of the interior throughout the 1930s and 1940s and into the 1950s (Swain 170, 244–48, 260, 275–76).

Albright also held a prominent and highly visible position among wilderness preservation groups. In the following, Swain (1970) describes Albright's involvement in the wilderness preservation community:

> He [Albright] served as a member of the executive board of the American Planning and Civic Association, and in 1938 became its president. He went on the board of the National Association of Audubon Societies. He devoted considerable time to the advisory board of the American Game Association. At the invitation of chairman William B. Greeley, a New York attorney and conservationist, he participated in the affairs of the Conservation Committee of the Camp Fire Club of America. Of course, he continued his long association with the Boone and Crockett Club of New York and the Sierra Club of California. (255)

Albright would later serve as vice president of the American Pioneer Trails Association and the American Scenic and Historic Preservation Society (Swain 170, 288). He was also a councilor to the Save-the-Redwood League (Schrepfer 1983, 136). Given his leadership among these groups, Albright served as a conduit to coordinate political activity within the wilderness preservation community.

Albright's prominence both on national park issues and within the wilderness preservation community led to his appointment to several government bodies dealing with preservation issues and resource conservation matters. In the late 1940s, Albright was appointed to the Hoover Presidential Commission. The commission was charged with proposing a government reorganization plan. Albright was part of the commission's Task Force on Natural Resources (Swain 1970, 276). He was appointed in 1949 as trustee to the National Trust for Historic Preservation, which was entrusted "to coordinate efforts to preserve the nation's landmarks and shrines" (as quoted in Swain 1970, 288). In June 1952, he was appointed to the Advisory Board on National Parks, Historic Sites, Buildings, and Monuments (Swain 1970, 293). During the late 1950s, Albright became a member of the United States Geological Survey Advisory Board and the Advisory Council to the Outdoor Recreation Resources Review Commission (ORRRC) (Swain 1970, 306–7).

Throughout Albright's post–park service career, he maintained a close relationship with JDR Jr. Until JDR Jr.'s death in 1960, Albright and Rockefeller conferred on park service issues and wilderness preservation matters (Ernst 1991d). It was noted in the preceding chapter how Albright and JDR Jr. collaborated to help protect the leadership of the National Park Service from politically motivated appointments in 1953. Additionally, in late 1953, Albright alerted Rockefeller that proposed Interior Department appropriations for the national parks were going to be inadequate (Albright, 9 December 1953). Furthermore, Albright suspected strongly that the Interior Department's proposed park service budget would be substantially cut by the Bureau of the Budget, the precursor to the Office of Management and Budget. In light of this fear, Albright urged JDR Jr. to send a letter to President Eisenhower on this issue, and he did so. In his letter to the president, JDR Jr. explains:

> I have just read with deep concern the article in *Harper's Magazine* for October entitled, "Let's Close the National Parks." The writer of the article makes the suggestion to close the National Parks apparently as a last resort in order to prevent their further deterioration and impoverishment.
>
> Having over the years taken a deep interest in the creation, development and improvement of the National Parks, which afford infinite enjoyment to many millions of people every year, I cannot but feel that if the gravity of the present situation were fully realized, some way would be found to stem the tide of this national tragedy. (10 December 1953)

Later, in January 1954, Albright reported to JDR Jr. that the president, in his budget message to Congress, "made special reference to his recommended increase in funds for management and protection o[f] our national parks, monuments and historic sites." Albright went on to argue that "I feel confident that this vital increase in funds that has been recommended [by the president] would not have reached Congress . . . had it not been for your [JDR Jr.'s] direct intercession with the President" (25 January 1954).

Through his relationship with the park service, Albright would help Rockefeller resolve park service related issues (Ernst 1991d). The following excerpt aptly captures the relationship among Albright, JDR Jr. and the Park Service. In this letter Albright is explaining to Rockefeller how he is dealing with an issue that JDR Jr. raised concerning the Great Smoky Mountains National Park. He points out that "I am going to be in Washington [D.C.] from next Monday, the 27th, to February 9th and expect to interview National Park Service officials on a number of matters." He goes on to ask JDR Jr. "Are there any other matters bearing on the various park projects in which *we* are interested that I ought to inquire into while I am down there?" [emphasis added] (23 January 1947). JDR Jr.'s park projects would also become Albright's projects. Albright would, in turn, employ his influence with the park service, and throughout Washington, to have these projects implemented.

Albright's association with Rockefeller preservation projects also involved formal participation. Ernst (1991b) explains that "Albright's association with the Rockefellers included his service on the boards and commissions of the American Youth Hostel, Colonial Williamsburg, American Conservation Association, Jackson Hole Preserve, Inc., and the Palisades Interstate Park Commission" (19). It is to Jackson Hole, and Albright and JDR Jr.'s work on this issue, that I turn our attention to next.

JACKSON HOLE

Stephen Mather, the park service's first director (1917–1928), and Albright had sought to have the Jackson Hole area, located in Wyoming, incorporated into the national park system since 1916. Swain (1970) describes its scenic value in the following:

> The Tetons, rising abruptly along the fault line a few miles south of Yellowstone [National Park], are one of the most distinctive mountain ranges in the world. Jagged and ice-hewn, much like the High Sierra, these peaks surpass even the Swiss Alps in the grandeur of their natural setting. Juxtaposed against the high-rising Tetons is Jackson Hole, a stretch of rolling green meadows and flatlands running to the northeast toward Yellowstone, forming a spectacular valley. (114)

Most of this scenic land was under the control of the U.S. Forest Service. A legislative effort in 1919 to have Jackson Hole added to Yellowstone, however, failed.

This initial failure was coincided by the development of local opposition, especially among cattle firms, to the inclusion of Jackson Hole into the national park system. In 1919, this opposition culminated in the passage of a resolution by the Wyoming state legislature opposing the proposed expansion of Yellowstone's borders (Swain 1970, 115). The cattlemen who used the Jackson Hole region "were not a numerous host, also not prosperous" (Ise 1961, 496). These local ranchers, however, were aided in their opposition to the Jackson Hole project by cattlemen from throughout the state of Wyoming and in Congress. Ise describes rancher political power and their determination in opposing the Jackson Hole project: The "livestock men were strong in Congress—some of the senators and representatives from Wyoming and surrounding states were stockmen—and fought against the Jackson Hole with pertinacity" (496). Ise goes on to argue:

> One reason for this [opposition] was doubtless that these western livestock men always harbored a hope that they might be able to grab more land titles or leases if the land was not securely tied up in the park system. The [cattlemen's] associations spent a lot of time scheming to this end and their livestock men in Congress of course helped. They [ranchers] still had the old grab-bag theory, of the publicly owned lands. (496)

Rancher resistance to this park expansion dragged the Jackson Hole battle over a thirty-year period.

Historically, producer groups have been very successful in preventing the incorporation of public lands into the national park system, or the wilderness preserve system, that they deemed of economic worth. National park historian Alfred Runte (1973; 1997, chap. 3), in his review of the creation of national parks, concludes that, with few exceptions, those areas converted into national parks were "worthless" from the perspective of resource extraction. He points out that "national parks protected only such areas as were considered valueless for profitable lumbering, mining, grazing, or agriculture" (1973, 5). Runte (1997) also explains that "even later awareness about a growing need for wilderness, wildlife, and biological conservation did not change the primary criterion of preservation—national parks must begin worthless and remain worthless to survive" (55). Finally, Runte (1973) argues that an entire ideology of uselessness has historically dominated the process of national park creation: "Throughout the history of the national parks, the concept of 'useless' scenery has virtually determined which areas the nation would protect and how it would protect them" (5).

Through the Wilderness Act of 1964, Congress mandated the creation of wilderness areas. In these protected areas, timber harvesting, roads, and the use of motorized equipment is prohibited. Once an area is admitted into the wilderness system it can only be withdrawn through an act of Congress (Allin 1982). Those areas designated as wilderness under the Wilderness Act of 1964, however, had little economic value. National forest historian Paul Hirt (1994) points out that the nine million acres of national forest set aside as wilderness in the Wilderness Act "contained very little commercial timber"

(232). Furthermore, while the act prohibits timber extraction in wilderness zones, it allows livestock grazing, water development, and mining on valid claims (McCloskey 1966, 303–4, 311–12, and 319–20).[3]

In the case of wilderness preservation policies in Alaska, Runte found that the historic principle guiding federal preservation policy of protecting only economically marginal lands persisted. The cornerstone of federal wilderness preservation in Alaska is the Alaska Lands Act of 1980. Runte (1997) points out that "in park after park [created by the act], critical wildlife habitat had either been fragmented to accommodate resource extraction or excluded entirely" (255). Additionally, of the hundred million acres protected by the Alaska Lands Act, twenty million acres were only given the tenuous legal and political protection of "preserve" status. Runte (1997), after reviewing the administrative history of preserves, concludes that "Congress had granted wide discretion to the secretary of the interior to allow mining, oil drilling, grazing, hunting, trapping, and other extractive uses both within and adjacent to [preserve] parks" (256). Moreover, he goes on to explain that "the mountainous, inaccessible landscapes forming the core of the new parks and monuments [in Alaska] rarely had the same potential for economic development" as did the preserves (256). Finally, the most economically viable areas of the state, "especially along the seacoasts . . . and . . . the forests of its southeastern panhandle," were left open to economic development (Runte 1997, 256).

Given the federal government's history of aversion to preserving lands of economic value, how did the Jackson Hole area ultimately become part of the national park system? The answer is John D. Rockefeller, Jr. and Horace Albright. It was their collaborative effort that brought the Jackson Hole area into the national park system, despite the opposition of politically and economically powerful special interests.

John D. Rockefeller, Jr. and Jackson Hole

JDR Jr. first became interested in the Jackson Hole area when he, with his wife and children, visited Yellowstone National Park in July 1926. On this trip, Albright, who at the time was Yellowstone Park superintendent, escorted JDR Jr. and his family around the park. Albright guided them out to the Jackson Hole area, where the Rockefellers expressed dismay at the commercial development in the area, which in their estimation marred "this glorious country" (as quoted in Swain 1970, 156). Albright explained to them that the development in the area, which included "a dilapidated gasoline station, a tawdry dance hall, and a cluster of nondescript cabins along the road," was on private land (Swain 1970, 156). At that point, JDR Jr. became interested in obtaining these private lands for the ultimate purpose of preserving the entire area and having it incorporated into the national park system. He asked Albright for an estimate on the costs of purchasing the private lands in Jackson Hole (Swain 1970, 156).

Albright knew that, in addition to political opposition, the privately held lands in the Jackson Hole area posed another obstacle to its incorporation into the national park system. As early as 1923, Albright and several local residents had hoped to raise, though private donations, the funds necessary to purchase these private holdings. By 1926, however, only a few thousand dollars had been obtained (Swain 1970, 156; Righter 1982, 34). Additionally, in the early 1920s another attempt to resolve the Jackson Hole situation also failed. A coordinating committee was appointed by two federal commissions: the President's Outdoor Recreation Committee and the Jackson Hole Elk Commission (Swain 1970, 156). This coordinating committee was unable "to bring the warring factions in Jackson together" (Swain 1970, 157). Therefore, Rockefeller's interest in the Jackson Hole area represented potentially the first major positive step toward achieving Albright's objective of protecting Jackson Hole.

In November 1926, Albright traveled to New York City to present to JDR Jr. his proposal for Jackson Hole. JDR Jr. however, rejected Albright's proposal, because he felt it was not ambitious enough. Instead, JDR Jr. envisioned a project that encompassed both sides of the Snake River. Albright's original proposal cost a projected $250,000, while the Rockefeller inspired proposal had projected costs of $1,000,000. Shortly after Albright modified his proposal to reflect JDR Jr.'s ambitions, Rockefeller agreed to undertake the project (Swain 1970, 160–61).

On 7 July 1927, President Calvin Coolidge withdrew the federally owned land in Jackson Hole. This presidential action took place shortly after Kevin Chorley, an assistant to JDR Jr. explained Rockefeller's plans to Hubert Work, secretary of the interior, and William B. Greeley, chief of the forest service. Work acknowledged that the withdrawal had occurred because of the "suggestion of Mr. Chorley of New York" (as quoted in Righter 1982, 54). The withdrawal of the federal lands in Jackson Hole allowed the JDR Jr. plan to proceed, and on 23 August 1927, the Snake River Land Company began to make land purchases in the area. This company was organized to help conceal Rockefeller's plans and his involvement, because if both of these facts were known it would have substantially inflated land prices in the area. By 1933, JDR Jr. had purchased approximately 35,000 acres in Jackson Hole at a cost of about $1,400,000 (Ise 1961, 494; Swain 1970, 162–63; Righter 1982, chap. 4).

Swain (1970) points out, that beginning soon after Albright resigned from the National Park Service, "In cooperation with Harold Fabian, Kenneth Chorley, and Vanderbilt Webb, all associated with Rockefeller, Albright kept lobbying for a Jackson Hole settlement" (253). Despite Albright's efforts and Rockefeller's willingness to turn his lands over to the park service at no cost, the federal government did not accept this gift (Swain 1970, 261; Righter 1982, chap. 6). Opposition to the Jackson Hole project successfully prevented the creation of a park in Jackson Hole and prevented the federal government from accepting JDR Jr.'s land. This opposition was centered in Wyoming and in Congress. In 1934, a compromise bill promoted by Albright passed the Senate but failed in the House (Swain 1970, 252). With the failure of this bill, Swain (1970) explains that "never again during the 1930s was the Rockefeller–Albright plan for preserving the Jackson Hole region so close to realization" (253). In early 1939, the Wyoming state legislature approved a resolution asking Congress to prevent the passage of legislation that would authorize the "purchase or acceptance as a gift by the United States or any of its agencies, of privately owned lands in Teton County, Wyoming," where Jackson Hole is located (as quoted in Swain 1970, 254).

In November 1942, JDR Jr. wrote Secretary of the Interior Harold Ickes about his Jackson Hole property. In this letter Rockefeller explained:

> In view of the uncertainty of the times, like everybody else I am and have been for some time reducing my obligations and burdens in so far as I wisely can. In line with that policy I have definitely reached the conclusion, although most reluctantly, that I should make permanent disposition of this [Jackson Hole] property before another year has passed. If the Federal Government is not interested in its acquisition, or, being interested, is still unable to arrange to accept it on the general terms long discussed and with which you are familiar, it will be my thought to make some other disposition of it or, failing in that, to sell it in the market to any satisfactory buyers. (27 November 1942)

JDR Jr. also wrote President Roosevelt explaining his dilemma (10 February 1943), hoping that the president would create a national monument in the Jackson Hole area. This idea was suggested by Kenneth Chorley, Rockefeller's assistant (Swain 1970, 262; Righter 1982, 103–5).

Under the Lacey Act of 1906, the president could unilaterally create a national monument of an area that had historic or scientific significance. This has the effect of creating a national park without having to gain the approval of Congress.[4] In a letter to Ickes, dated 5 January 1943, JDR Jr. exhorts the secretary to have the president declare the national monument despite the expected political backlash:

> During the course of our talk you made it clear that it is your intention at an early date to bring to the President for his signature the order for the incorporation as a National Monument of both public and private property within the Jackson Hole area, thus rounding out the Grand Teton Park project. While we were in agreement that such action on the President's part may call forth some criticism, both political and local, we were fully in accord in believing that because this proposition is so eminently sound and so wholly in the interest of the American people, such criticism would quickly die down and would be followed shortly, even on the part of the objectors, by general approval of the President's action.

On 15 March 1943, FDR issued an executive order creating the Jackson Hole National Monument (Ise 1961, 498; Swain 1970, 262–63; Righter 1982, 103–10).

The president's action, however, did not end the battle over Jackson Hole (Righter 1982, chap. 7). Immediately after the creation of the Jackson Hole National Monument, the Barrett Bill was submitted to Congress. This bill would have abolished the monument. The Barrett Bill was passed by Congress in late 1943; however, it was pocket-vetoed by the president (Ise 1961, 498–504; Swain 1970, 266). While the Barrett Bill was unsuccessful, congressional opponents of the Jackson Hole project were able to attach to every Interior Department appropriation bill from 1944 to 1948 an amendment that forbade any expenditures on the Jackson Hole Monument (Ise 1961, 505; Righter 1982, 123). This prevented the park service from taking control of the monument and JDR Jr.'s property.

The stalemate over Jackson Hole continued until 1947. When the Republicans took control over both branches of Congress in 1946, opponents of the national monument felt confident that the Barrett Bill could again be passed (Swain 1970, 281). Swain explains that "once again, as in 1943 and 1944, Albright became one of the leaders of the small but influential group of conservationists who battled the Barrett Bill" (1970, 281). Albright argued that the opponents of the bill should not count on a presidential veto but instead should employ the "hard-hitting strategy of opposing the Barrett Bill strenuously at every stage of the legislative process" (Swain 1970, 282).

Albright mobilized and coordinated the political opposition to the Barrett Bill. He managed these individuals with the help of Rockefeller associates Kenneth Chorley and Harold Fabian (Swain 1970, 282). Swain describes Albright's mobilization and coordination efforts in the following:

> He [Albright] obtained the help of R. R. M. Carpenter, a member of the Boone and Crockett and the vice-president of DuPont, and Lionel Weil, an influential North Carolina businessman, in lining up opposition to the [Barrett] bill. He [Albright] acted as coordinator and middleman between H. E. Anthony of the Boone and Crockett Club, John Baker of the National Audubon Society, and Marshall McLeon of the Camp Fire Club, who rounded up congressmen willing to object to the Barrett Bill when it came up on the consent calendar. Every possible contact was explored. Albright even called upon his old friend and classmate Earl Warren, now governor of California, to join the fight. (282–83)

Swain goes on to point out that "by painstaking effort and fast footwork the Rockefeller group [of Albright, Chorley, and Fabian] bottled up the Barrett Bill" in the House Public Lands Committee (283).

With the realization that the Barrett Bill was not going to make it out of committee, its congressional proponents turned to the House Rules Committee. They hoped that this committee would introduce the bill to the full House (Swain 1970, 283). Albright then, too, turned to the Rules Committee. In addition to his own personal lobbying efforts, Albright again mobilized many of the same preservationists, and political allies, to pressure the Rules Committee that he did in defeating the Barrett Bill in the Public Lands Committee (Swain 1970, 283). Swain explains that "by the spring of 1948, it was clear that the Barrett Bill would never reach the House floor. Unmourned and virtually unnoticed, the bill to abolish the Jackson Hole National Monument languished and finally died" (283).

With the death of the Barrett Bill in 1948, opponents of the Jackson Hole project decided to compromise. A compromise was negotiated by the Wyoming congressional delegation, the National Park Service, the Jackson Hole Preserve, Inc., and the state of Wyoming (Swain 1970, 284; Righter 1982, 138). Jackson Hole Preserve, Inc., was an entity created by JDR Jr. to manage his Jackson Hole property. The compromise legislation, entitled the O'Mahoney–Hunt Bill, added two hundred thousand acres of the Jackson Hole area to Grand Teton National Park. Approximately six thousand acres of the monument went to the adjoining National Elk Refuge, and three thousand acres were allocated to the Grand Teton National Forest (Ise 1961, 506). The legislation also protected the grazing rights of those cattlemen in the area (Swain 1970, 284; Righter 1982, 138). Ise argues that "the lease continuance provisions for stockmen and for owners of summer homes, were exceedingly generous to lessees, amounting almost to possible perpetual leases" (507).

The compromise bill, officially entitled "A New Grand Teton National Park," was signed by President Truman on 14 September 1950 (Ise 1961, 506; Righter 1982, 140). Shortly before the passage of the O'Mahoney–Hunt Bill, the park service accepted JDR Jr.'s gift of land (Righter 1982, 139). With this acceptance, and the subsequent incorporation of the Jackson Hole area into the national park system, JDR Jr. and Albright's objective was finally achieved.

CONCLUSION

The preservation of the Jackson Hole area conforms to the economic elite model of public policymaking. In other words, wealthy actors, utilizing their wealth and/or prestige, played central and determining roles in the policymaking process that incorporated the Jackson Hole area into the national park system.[5] It was JDR Jr.'s lobbying efforts in the 1920s that prompted the president to withdraw the public lands in the area. Rockefeller used his wealth as a political resource by purchasing private lands in the Jackson Hole area and then by offering them to the park service. Additionally, JDR Jr. personally intervened in the early 1940s with the secretary of the interior and President Roosevelt to break a seemingly insurmountable impasse. This intervention had the effect of creating the Jackson Hole National Monument. Albright, himself a high-level member of the corporate community and acting in significant part as JDR Jr.'s agent, used his position as a leader in the wilderness preservation community to defeat the opponents of the Jackson Hole project in Congress. Together, Albright and JDR Jr. defeated the politically potent special interests that opposed the Jackson Hole project. In doing so, they brought an area whose natural resources were economically viable into the national park system, a rarity in federal wilderness preservation history.

Finally, the recession of Yosemite Park and the incorporation of the Jackson Hole area into the national park system provide us with insight into how the wilderness preservation community has historically influenced the development of federal wilderness preservation policy. Specifically, these cases elucidate how economic elites have mediated the relationship between the wilderness preservation community and wilderness preservation policy. In the case of Yosemite Park, it was the economic elites that owned and managed the Southern Pacific Railroad, informed by the wilderness activists of the Sierra Club, that precipitated the park's recession to the federal government. With regard to Jackson Hole, it was an economic elite leader within the wilderness preservation community, Horace Albright, who marshaled important members of this community behind a plan initiated and financed by another economic elite, JDR Jr. This relationship between economic elites and the wilderness preservation community indicates that substantial portions of the wilderness preservation community have historically operated as an economic elite–led policy-planning network. Did this relationship, and the dominant role of economic elites in the development of wilderness preservation policy, change in the 1960s when the public's awareness of wilderness and environmental issues grew exponentially? It is to these issues that I turn in the following chapter.

NOTES

1. This sum does not include the money Rockefeller provided for the development and preservation of Colonial Williamsburg (Ernst 1991b, 4).

2. Cammerer initially declined this $1,000 gift because of the appearance it created. After this refusal, through correspondence, Albright informed JDR Jr. that if the gift were routed through Cammerer's wife it could be accepted. I am assuming that Rockefeller did as Albright suggested (Rockefeller, 19 July 1939; Albright, 22 July 1939).

3. The Wilderness Act of 1964 prohibits the creation of mining claims in "wilderness areas" under the leasing and mining laws after 31 December 1983. The act, however, allows prospecting within wilderness areas indefinitely (McCloskey 1966).

4. See Ise (1961, 154–55) for a discussion of the vague distinction between a national "park" and a national "monument."

5. One could argue that Albright's prestige and the influence he wielded on the Jackson Hole issue were not wholly derived from his wealth, but in large part from his government service. Albright's park service and post–park service career is an excellent example of the reverse colonization of the state, however. In such cases, officials use their positions within it to service economic elite policy preferences with the implicit or explicit understanding that by doing so they will be rewarded with wealth and a

high-level corporate position upon leaving government. In turn, these former government officials will often use their prestige and government contacts derived from their government service to forward economic elite policy preferences. In this way, former government officials are incorporated within the economic elite, and economic elites use the prestige and other resources accumulated by former government officials to achieve their policy goals.

5

~

Anatomy of a Wilderness Controversy
The Creation of Redwood National Park

The cases of Yosemite Park and Jackson Hole indicate the central role that economic elites have historically played in federal wilderness preservation policy. Was this influence, however, as important during the 1960s when the public in large measure developed an acute concern for wilderness and the environment? This heightened awareness is reflected in the substantial expansion in membership that wilderness and environmental groups experienced during this period (Ingram and Mann 1989, 136–42; Lowry 1998, 47). The controversial and contentious creation of Redwood National Park in 1968 offers a good venue to determine whether the public's environmental activism of the 1960s displaced economic elites from their dominant position over federal wilderness preservation policy. The battle over the redwood park precipitated a battle between the economic elite–led Save-the-Redwood League and the Sierra Club, which by the mid-1960s was relying on broad-based support to achieve its political goals.

The Redwood National Park is located in coastal northern California, near the Oregon border. It entails a relatively small sliver of a redwood forest that runs along the coast of California from the Monterey peninsula to the Oregon border. This forest is primarily composed of redwoods whose scientific designation is *Sequoia sempervirens*. The other variant of the redwood tree is known as *Sequoiadendron gigantea*. While the *gigantea* redwood is widely known for the large circumference of its trunk, its wood is of poor quality for commercial use. In contrast, the redwood *sempervirens*, which is the tallest species of tree in the world, produces wood of high commercial value. As a result of its commercial value, the redwood *sempervirens*, or the coastal redwood, has historically been harvested by timber interests. Susan R. Schrepfer (1983) chronicles the history of the fight to preserve certain portions of the coastal redwood forest.

THE SAVE-THE-REDWOOD LEAGUE

The Save-the-Redwood League was established in 1918. Since its founding, the league has sought to protect those portions of the coastal redwood forest that have had scenic and/or scientific value. The Save-the-Redwood League was the brainchild of Madison Grant, Henry Fairfield Osborn, and John Campbell Merriam. All three had scientific backgrounds (Schrepfer 1983, 3–5). Grant, however, in addition to being a scientist was a New York patrician who "had inherited wealth that allowed him to be an amateur natural scientist and to help found the New York Zoological Society, the American Bison Society, and the Boone and Crockett Club" (Schrepfer 1983, 4).

The three had resolved to help preserve the coastal redwood forest when on an expedition in 1917 they realized the extent of infiltration that timber firms had made into the forest. In establishing the Save-the-Redwood League, Grant, Osborn, and Merriam not only sought out other scientists and preservation activists, but they successfully recruited wealthy individuals who could underwrite the organization and its goals. When, on 2 August 1919, seven league activists converged in San Francisco's Palace Hotel to elect officers, among them were borax industrialist and National Park Service director Stephen Mather and California petroleum and hydroelectric entrepreneur J. D. Grant (Schrepfer 1983, 13).

Throughout the Save-the-Redwood League's history, its connection to the corporate community and the upper class has been maintained. Between 1920 and 1939, the league had seventy-nine councilors. Its council is responsible for choosing its board of directors. Schrepfer (1983, 13–17) analyzed the background of these councilors. Ten were female; one of these women was an easterner, and the rest were wealthy residents of Los Angeles and San Francisco. They were all active in such women's civic organizations as the Garden Club of America and the California Federation of Women's Clubs. Both of these groups contributed to the league. The sixty-nine male councilors during this period were prominent professionals or businessmen (Schrepfer 1983, 14). Twenty-seven of the councilors were businessmen, in industries ranging from banking to manufacturing. Schrepfer points out that "the businessmen were prosperous pillars of the community—university regents, college controllers, and corporate directors" (14).

The high level of economic elite participation on Save-the-Redwood League's council has been maintained throughout its history, primarily because the league's councilors are self-perpetuating. In other words, the council is responsible for reelecting council members and for choosing replacements when an opening on the council does occur (Schrepfer 1983, 22). Schrepfer argues that "as intended by its founders, the organization's closed internal governance . . . provided stability" (113). She goes on to assert that "this stability made for moderation, as did the tendency for the council and board to be increasingly dominated by businessmen and patricians, while fewer academics were drawn into the organization's leadership in the 1950s and 1960s" (113).

In addition to the contributions and leadership that these wealthy councilors provided to the Save-the-Redwood League, they utilized their relationships with other individuals of wealth to obtain the political and economic resources necessary to save the redwoods. Schrepfer describes their efforts in fund raising: "These councilors quietly solicited donations in the exclusive haunts of New York's Sphinx Club; Washington, D.C.'s Cosmos Club; and California's Bohemian Club" (21). Furthermore, wealthy councilors "escorted potential benefactors down the Redwood Highway in a black, open-top touring car, encouraging these prominent citizens to select and name a memorial grove for family or friend" (Schrepfer 1983, 21). These memorials accounted for one-third of the league's money raised in the 1920s (Schrepfer 1983, 21). By touting the scientific and scenic value of the coastal redwoods among the nation's economic elite, wealthy councilors not only obtained the financing needed to save the redwoods but invariably gained goodwill for the redwood preservation project.

Therefore, the Save-the-Redwood League was the product of an alliance between academic "reformers" and "civic-minded" businesspeople (Schrepfer 1983, 28). Within this alliance, however, the businesspeople were not passive benefactors. Schrepfer argues that "between 1923 and 1927 the league was forced to thread a course between unyielding industrial interests to the right and park radicals to left" (25). "Park radicals" were those who placed the preservation of wilderness above corporate property rights. Schrepfer goes on to argue that the league's "reformers rode such a fine line in part out of fear that benefactors might close their wallets" (25). Historian Michael Cohen (1988) explains, "[Newton] Drury [the league's executive secretary] needed to make the League appear decorous, moderate, civilized, and politically conservative, or he could not attract the kind of money he needed [to preserve the redwoods]. He carefully avoided offending any future benefactors" (53). Schrepfer avers, however, that the "league's [accomodationist] inclination sprang more directly from the values of its councilors" (25).

The league's respect for corporate property rights can be seen in the case of its first major legislative activity. In 1921, it supported a preservation bill in the California legislature that was designed to accommodate the Pacific Lumber Company (Schrepfer 1983, 23–25). A bill was initially introduced in the legislature that would have empowered the State Board of Forestry to seize timberlands adjacent to the highway in Humboldt County. This bill, entitled the Redwood Preservation Bill, would have allowed the State Board of Forestry to condemn timberland under the ownership of the Pacific Lumber Company. This firm was the "owner of the finest [redwood] groves" along the highway. The bill was supported by the "organized and newly enfranchised" women in Humboldt County and by the "largest affected landowner—a corporate speculator" (Schrepfer 1983, 24). The league withdrew its support for the Redwood Preservation Bill, however, when it came "under fire from the timbermen's trade association" (Schrepfer 1983, 24). With the league's support, a bill that exempted the Pacific Lumber Company lands was passed to save the redwoods along the highway in Humboldt County.

The wealthy leaders and benefactors of the league also affected the political discourse it adhered to. Despite the affinity between the means of the league and the New Deal, the league was overtly hostile to the New Deal (Schrepfer 1983, chap. 5). Both the league and the New Deal sought to use the state's authority to achieve policy goals. It was the league's opposition to the New Deal that in part explains its opposition to the creation of a redwood national park in 1938 (Schrepfer 1983, 65). Schrepfer explains that "the league's ideological opposition to the New Deal resulted in part from its financial base" (74). She goes on to describe this financial base in the 1930s:

> By 1940 public funding accounted for over half of the redwoods saved, but the organization had to raise matching private subscriptions. Such of its memorials as the Children's Forest, originally dedicated to deceased children, accommodated small donations, but its funding success depended upon large gifts. In 1939, for example, 189 persons gave 13 percent of the funding for the Avenue of the Giants; the remainder came from only five individuals. Inclusion of John D. Rockefeller, Jr.'s two million dollar donation in the 1930s for Bull Creek Flat in Humboldt Redwoods State Park further diminishes the significance of the small gift. (74)

Schrepfer concludes by contending that "dependence upon the rich and well-born and believers in rugged individualism . . . contributed to the league's anti–New Deal stance" (74). The American Forestry Association, the National Parks Association, and the Sierra Club, all preservation and/or resource conservation groups, also adopted anti–New Deal perspectives (Schrepfer 1983, 73).

Despite the league's anti–New Deal position, Secretary of the Interior Harold Ickes offered the position of National Park Service director twice to Newton Drury, the league's executive secretary—in 1934 and again in 1939. Drury rejected it in 1934 but accepted it in 1939. As noted in the preceding chapter, many members within the Save-the-Redwood League embraced the "purist" preservationist view of the national parks. Drury's outlook reflected this purist perspective (Ise 1961, 443–44; Swain 1970, 259; Schrepfer 1983, 54; Hartzog 1988, 81–83). His opinions on national park management did not immediately create conflict with "use" preservationists, however, because Drury's tenure (1940–1951) as park service director coincided with the war and economic recovery (Ise 1961, 447–48; Sellars 1997, chap. 5). In 1951, however, Secretary of the Interior Oscar Chapman demanded Drury's resignation. Horace Albright was allowed to mediate his departure from the park service. As a result, Drury resigned from the park service in a timely manner and simultaneously assumed the position of director of California State Parks and Beaches (Swain 1970, 290–91). In 1959, Drury returned to the league, as its executive secretary (Schrepfer 1983, 113).

The league's anti–New Deal and purist predilections prevented the creation of a redwood national park in the interim between the wars, when the national park system was significantly expanded (Schrepfer 1983, chap. 5). With a soft timber market during this period (Robbins 1982), the coastal redwoods were not under immediate threat. During the post–World War II boom, however, the redwoods came under increasing pressure (Schrepfer 1983, 108–9 and 111; Cohen 1988, 301). In the 1960s, timber harvesting in the area prompted the league to ask the federal government to create a redwood national park. At this time, however, the league's leadership in the effort to preserve the coastal redwood was challenged by a transformed and aggressive Sierra Club.

THE SIERRA CLUB AND DAVID BROWER

Between the Hetch Hetchy battle of the 1900s (Jones 1965) and the 1950s, the Sierra Club refrained from high-profile political battles. During this interim, the club was predominately focused on helping its members enjoy the Sierra Mountains. Furthermore, the club, and its leadership, collaborated closely with the park service and the forest service during this period. Additionally, the club discreetly managed political disagreements (Cohen 1988, chaps. 1–3).

Under the leadership of David Bower, however, the Sierra Club adopted an increasingly contentious, and national, profile on wilderness issues. By the mid-1960s, it was openly critical of corporate America and the land management practices of the federal government. Also, when the battle to create a redwood national park came to a head, the club was running significantly to the left of the Save-the-Redwood League (Schrepfer 1983, chap. 9; Cohen 1988, chap. 6).

Bower became the executive director of the Sierra Club in 1952—the first in its history. Initially, Brower appeared to be a "safe" choice for executive director. The leadership of the Sierra Club in the 1950s was guided by what can be referred to as "traditional" notions of wilderness preservation. Specifically, this has meant that only those portions of the wilderness that had scientific and/or scenic value should be preserved. Historically, traditional wilderness preservation in the United States has also meant that the preservation of wilderness should not interfere with economic development.

Like the league, the club's notions of wilderness were rooted in the social and economic background of its leadership. The club leadership, by the 1920s, was predominantly composed of businesspeople (Orsi 1985; Cohen 1988, 51). In describing the outlook of the club leadership beginning in the 1920s, Sierra Club historian Michael Cohen (1988) explains:

> These men were immersed professionally and personally in the economic growth of California, not wealthy yet, but the prime movers in what one might call the philanthropic tradition of conservation, where business provided the individuals, progressivism provided the ideology, and American industrial growth provided the economic power. (51–52)

Hence, when the club's board members chose Brower as the organization's executive director, they felt that he shared their thoughts on the importance of economic growth, their limited concept of wilderness preservation, and the importance of corporate America to the achievement of wilderness preservation goals.

Little in Brower's background would have ostensibly suggested he would deviate from traditional wilderness preservation. Brower, born in 1912, had worked as publicity director for Yosemite Park and the Curry Company in the 1930s, and in the 1940s he was an editor at the University of California Press. He had worked with the club several years without incident before his appointment as executive director. He served as a board member for twelve years. In addition, Brower edited the club's periodical, the *Bulletin*, and established the *Sierra Club Handbook* in 1947 (Cohen 1988, 150). Despite this history, Brower became in many people's eyes a radical environmentalist, and in many important respects he took the club with him.

THE SIERRA CLUB IN THE 1950s AND 1960s

The Sierra Club reentered the national scene because of the Upper Colorado River Basin Project proposed in 1950. This project, which included two dams and reservoirs, would have flooded the Dinosaur National Monument in Utah. With the prospect that the national park system might be violated, the club and David Brower took the lead in fighting the proposed flooding of the monument. The club's board of directors restricted Brower to a narrowly construed argument to preserve the monument. Brower, and others associated with the club, sought a multifaceted attack on the Upper Colorado project. They wanted to oppose the entire project—specifically, its proposed flooding of areas not under the protection of the national park system. Additionally, Brower wanted to critique the economic feasibility of the entire Upper Colorado project. By inference, this critique would have impugned the creditability of the

Bureau of Reclamation, the agency that proposed the project, and its motives. This strategy would have placed the club in the position of opposing a large development project in the West. Instead, the board dictated to Brower that he and the club only oppose the flooding of Dinosaur Monument and that this opposition be based on the protection of the sanctity of the national park system, not on implicit critiques of the Bureau of Reclamation or the economic feasibility of the project (Cohen 1988, chap. 4). Cohen explains that "when the Club chose not to confront the whole Upper Colorado project or the powerful corporate forces behind it, this was partly because many Club members were not opposed to developing the West, were not even opposed to federal subsidies providing water for the arid West" (176). These club members, and their views, were well represented on the board of directors. Ultimately, the club, and other preservation groups, were successful in preventing the flooding of the Dinosaur National Monument (Harvey 1991; Winks 1997, 88).

While Brower remained within the constraints laid down by the club's board during the Dinosaur Monument controversy, tension and confrontations eventually developed between Brower and many board members, especially those who operated within the traditional paradigm of wilderness preservation. Part of the disagreement between Brower and the board arose because he publicly criticized the federal government, specifically the U.S. Forest Service, for its management of the national forests (Cohen 1988, 232 and 234, chap. 5). Many of the more influential board members, however, sought to discreetly negotiate with the forest service over policy disagreements (Cohen 1988, 204–11). Brower, in contrast, adopted the perspective that "diplomacy, perfection of techniques for getting along, will accomplish a great deal. It will not, however, save what can only be saved by fighting" (as quoted in Cohen 1988, 235). After articles were published in the club's periodical, the *Bulletin*, "Impugning the motives of public officials" (as quoted in Cohen 1988, 232), the club's board passed a resolution in December 1959 entitled "Relations with Public Agencies." This resolution pronounced that "no statement should be used [by the Club] that expressly, impliedly, or by reasonable inference criticizes the motives, integrity, or competence of an official or bureau" (as quoted in Cohen 1988, 237).

A more central, and intractable, source of conflict between Brower and many Sierra Club board members was based on philosophy. Specifically, Brower began to prioritize wilderness and the environment over economic growth and development. This placed him at odds with many of the "old-line" preservationists on the board. Brower's conflict with certain members of the club's board manifested itself in disputes over policy goals and the scope and content of the club's publication program (Cohen 1988, chaps. 6, 7, and 8).

Under Brower's leadership, the Sierra Club itself began to change (Schrepfer 1983, 107). For instance, the club's membership throughout the 1950s and 1960s grew exponentially. When the club's Dinosaur campaign began in 1952, its membership stood at seven thousand. By 1967, this figure was at fifty-five thousand (Cohen 1988, 275). This membership reflected the growth of the club's national stature, as well as the stature of David Brower (McPhee 1970; Cohen 1988, 275, 292, and 295). The increase in membership, and membership dues, was required by Brower to pursue his environmental campaigns. In contrast to the Save-the-Redwood League, which needs substantial funds to acquire redwood groves, the club relied historically on membership dues to cover its operating expenses.

The composition of the club's board of directors also changed significantly. Unlike the Save-the-Redwood League, the Sierra Club's board members are chosen by the general membership. As a result, Brower was able to have many individuals nominated and elected to the board (Cohen 1988, 275). These new board members were more receptive to his approach to wilderness issues. Hence, by the 1960s, the board as a whole was more supportive of Brower's goals and means (Schrepfer 1983, 178; Cohen 1988, 275, and 340). Schrepfer points out that many of the board members elected in the 1960s had significantly weaker ties to the corporate community than did the old-line board members: "It can be noted that this [new] group [of club board members] was generally younger and none had the strong, professional interaction with business of [old guard board members] [Richard] Leonard, Bestor Robinson, or Alex Hildebrand" (178). The old-line preservationists, however, did retain a significant presence on the board (Cohen 1988, 340). In 1969, these board members took a leading role in orchestrating Brower's ouster from his executive director position. They were able to do so, in large part, because of his alleged mismanagement of the club's finances (Schrepfer 1983, 182–83; Cohen 1988, chap. 8).

Under Brower's stewardship, the club also changed its political strategy. To achieve the club's goals, Brower sought to wield its sizable membership and following as a cudgel against recalcitrant politicians. This approach yielded confrontation and conflict with public officials and competing interest groups. Through this confrontation and conflict Brower hoped to achieve the club's policy goals (Schrepfer 1983, 108 and chap. 9). Thus, he and the Sierra Club in the 1960s put into practice the pluralist model of policymaking described in the 1950s and early 1960s by such political theorists as David Truman (1951) and Robert Dahl (1961). Brower felt that he could use a mobilized and growing membership, and their votes, to force political officials and corporate America into making significant and substantial concessions.

Prior to the ascension of Brower, the club relied on a political strategy that is more indicative of C. Wright Mills's (1956) power elite perspective, also formulated in the 1950s. Old-line club leaders believed that policy goals were most efficaciously reached through quiet cooperation with political and corporate elites (Schrepfer 1983, 171). For example, Cohen (1988) describes the attitude of longtime club leader and board member Bestor Robinson toward the club's relationship with government leaders in the following: He "continued to believe that the Club's strength depended on the friends it could keep in [federal land management] agencies, even if that required accommodating philosophies unlike or even conflicting with those of the Club" (206). Another longtime board member, Richard Leonard, "preferred a personal and conversational style of negotiation with the heads of federal agencies" (206). Schrepfer states that "prior to the 1960s club leaders . . . had found . . . an effective conservation strategy in service on boards advisory to the departments of the Interior and of Agriculture and such agencies as the National Park Service and the Forest Service" (171). She also explains that "older leaders . . . argued that the club should use liberally inclined industrialists and businessmen as sources of expertise, influence, and philanthropy" (171).

Joel Hildebrand, a club director from the 1930s to 1965, described the change in the club's politics. He explained the board of directors, traditionally composed of "men of influence," would "alert all their friends in the East to apply pressure" when needed. Hildebrand went on to grouse that under Brower the club came to represent: "Voters, voting strength, and no official . . . wants to alienate a good many thousand of voters. . . . Our strength earlier was moral strength . . . and cogent argument rather than threats and confrontation" (as quoted in Schrepfer 1983, 175–76 [author's ellipses]). Brower also acknowledged the club's changing political strategy. He rhetorically asked, "Should we be bold or should we be diplomats?" and answered:

> Private diplomacy belonged in the Bohemian Club [an elite social club] but it didn't belong in the Sierra Club. We were trying to get the public to move, and the Bohemian Club type of operation [which the club had historically practiced] is trying to get the leaders to move. (as quoted in Schrepfer 1983, 176; Cohen 1988, 206)

The Save-the-Redwood League uses the "Bohemian Club" approach to political disputes (Schrepfer 1983). In describing the difference between the club and league, Cohen (1988) explains that by the mid-1960s "the Club was very different from the League as a conservation organization: the Club would use the public as a force, [it] would not look for wealthy connections" (310). During the mid-1960s, the league and the club utilized their disparate political resources in the battle to determine the location and size of a redwood national park.

THE REDWOOD NATIONAL PARK ACT OF 1968

By 1963, the Save-the-Redwood League's conservative approach to wilderness preservation had resulted in the creation of four high-quality state redwood parks, located in northern California: the Jedediah Smith Redwoods State Park, the Del Norte Coast Redwoods State Park, Prairie Creek Redwoods State Park, and the Humboldt Redwoods State Park. These parks encompassed 102,000 acres of redwood forest lands and were valued at over $11 million (Schrepfer 1983, 113).

In became apparent by the mid-1950s, however, that the league's approach of preserving only those areas of scientific and scenic value, as well as those areas that produced least political resistance, had yielded parks that were unviable. Accelerated timber harvesting in the redwood belt threatened the redwood, including those in state parks. Schrepfer (1983) points out that by the late 1950s "only about 10 percent of the original two million-acre redwood belt remained uncut" (111). Timber harvesting near the state parks made the redwoods within them vulnerable to soil erosion. The redwood, with its shallow roots, is especially sensitive to soil erosion.[1]

Humboldt Redwoods State Park, for example, was severely damaged in the 1950s by nearby logging activity. The park was part of the Bull Creek watershed. As a result of logging throughout the watershed, "Bull Creek grew muddy and wide" (Schrepfer 1983, 109). In the winter of 1954–1955, unusually heavy rains created flooding, and "piles of logs [created by timber firms] were swept up into the muddy, raging waters of Bull Creek to form battering rams" (Schrepfer 1983, 109). As described by Schrepfer, "By the time the waters abated, 525 giant redwoods had been lost from the Rockefeller Forest" within Humboldt Park (109).

In addition to the threat evident to the Humboldt State Park, as a result of logging activity "the league also worried about the safety of Mill Creek Flat in the heart of Del Norte County's Jedediah Smith Redwoods State Park" (Schrepfer 1983, 112). Schrepfer points out that as late as the latter 1950s, "Despite accelerated logging, the rise of in stumpage rates, the lumbermen's growing reluctance to sell land, and threatened park erosion, [the Save-the-Redwood League] continued to emphasize cooperation with industry as well as state and private reform" (113). She goes on to argue that "the league's constancy stemmed from the continued reinforcement of shared values of the leadership and donors" (113).

By 1960, however, the league had decided to accept federal help. The cost of continuing to acquire redwoods for preservation had become prohibitive for the league and its benefactors. This became especially the case as state funds for the redwood project dried up (Schrepfer 1983, 115). The league's idea for a national park, however, continued to be guided by its traditional approach to wilderness preservation. Newton Drury asserted in 1960:

> The same considerations we stated in the 1946 report are still pertinent to the question of the Redwood National Park: the four main projects of the League . . . represent the core of the areas of greatest caliber, worthy of being incorporated in a national park [author's ellipses]. (as quoted in Schrepfer 1983, 116)

The league's proposed national park would round out the Jedediah Smith Redwoods State Park and the Del Norte Coast Redwoods State Park. Its proposal was to convert the entire Mill Creek watershed (forty-two thousand acres) into a national park, much of which was already state park land (Schrepfer 1983, 114, 116, and 122).

Building on a park service plan for national redwood park, the Sierra Club proposed an ambitious park plan. The park service, rejecting the league's idea for a national park, instead proposed in 1964 a park of fifty-six thousand acres that would run along the Redwood Creek and encompass the Prairie Creek Redwoods State Park. The park service rejected the smaller Mill Creek proposal, in part, because the planned rebuilding of the freeways in the area undermined its park "worthiness" (Schrepfer 1983, 118–19, and 132). The club gravitated quickly toward the park service proposal. However, it proposed an even larger park in the Redwood Creek area. The club argued that the entire Redwood Creek watershed should be preserved as a national park; thus, they proposed a ninety-thousand-acre park that would encompass the whole watershed (Cohen 1988, 307 and 309).

The different proposals made by the league and the club reflected their decidedly different concepts of wilderness and its preservation. The league argued that the Mill Creek watershed contained a high quality redwood forest, much of it already publicly owned. Furthermore, the league pointed out that the park service proposed park contained redwood trees of inferior quality, and that other species of trees were mixed in with them (Schrepfer 1983, 121–22). In contrast, the club's proposal was designed to preserve ecosystems, not simply the redwood. The large park idea put forth by the club was designed to ensure ecological diversity and the unencumbered operation of ecosystems. Also, unlike the league, which believed in technological progress and economic development, many of the club's leaders by 1960s began to argue that ecosystems and ecological diversity should be protected at the expense of technological progress and economic development (Schrepfer 1983, 125–29; Cohen 1988, 310).

The differing proposals also reflected the organizations' contrasting political tactics. The league's national park effort sought to avoid the political ire of potent economic interest groups. The private land that the league's proposal would have incorporated into a national park was owned by a relatively small timber firm, the Miller Redwood Company. It was owned by Harold Miller, a "known maverick in the [logging] industry" (Schrepfer 1983, 138). The forest lands in Redwood Creek, in contrast, were held by financially and politically powerful firms. These firms were the Georgia–Pacific Corporation, the Simpson Timber Company, and the Arcata Redwood Company. Georgia–Pacific and Simpson were both major timber firms. Arcata was connected to the Weyerhaeuser timber empire (Hidy et al. 1963). Its chairman was C. Davis Weyerhaeuser, the son of Frederick Weyerhaeuser. Other board members included John J. Pascoe, the brother-in-law of George Weyerhaeuser, and Albert J. Morman, an attorney to many Weyerhaeuser family members (Schrepfer 1983,

138–39). Schrepfer argues that when the league's leaders choose the Mill Creek area as a site for a national park, in addition to being guided by their wilderness preservation philosophy, "They were also respon[ding] to the needs of the lumber industry and to the realities of financial power" (139). In contrast, the club leadership believed that by mobilizing the public they could impose a settlement (Schrepfer 1983, 134; Cohen 1988, 352–57).

Following the park service proposal, Secretary of the Interior Stewart Udall supported Redwood Creek as a site for a national park (Schrepfer 1983, 130). Despite the park service plan and the secretary's support for it, the Johnson White House in the summer of 1965 endorsed the league plan. The primary reason for Lyndon Johnson's embrace of the league plan was Laurance Rockefeller.

Laurance Rockefeller, beginning in the late 1940s, had taken up his father, JDR Jr.'s, interest in wilderness preservation and resource conservation issues (Collier and Horowitz 1976, 304–9; Winks 1997). Unlike JDR Jr. who limited his involvement in preservation issues to the contribution of funds and to consultation with government officials, Laurance assumed a direct governmental role in preservation matters. In 1958, President Eisenhower appointed Rockefeller to the chairpersonship of the Outdoor Recreation Resources and Review Commission (ORRRC) (Winks 1997, chap. 7). The purpose of ORRRC was to inventory the nation's recreational resources (Swain 1970, 307).[2] In 1964, Rockefeller was appointed by Johnson to his Task Force on Natural Beauty and, in 1965, as head of the White House Conference on Natural Beauty (Collier and Horowitz 1976, 386–87; Schrepfer 1983, 136; Winks 1997, chap. 8; Gould 1999, 37, 50–51 and 60). Collier and Horowitz explain that "one of the conference's results was the creation of a Citizen's Advisory Committee on Recreation and Natural Beauty, with Laurance serving as chairman and charged with advising the White House on environmental matters" (1976, 387; Winks 1997, 144 and 150). From 1969 to 1976, Laurence also served as the chairman to the presidential Citizen's Advisory Committee on Environmental Quality (Ernst 1991a, 340; Winks 1997, 155–56).

Laurance Rockefeller's support for the league's plan is not surprising given that the Rockefeller family had a long association with the Save-the-Redwood League. According to Collier and Horowitz (1976), Newton Drury had been a member of the Rockefellers' "outer circle" since the 1920s (149). JDR Jr. contributed $2 million to help the league preserve the redwood (Ernst 1991b). In addition, Horace Albright, one of the family's advisers on preservation and conservation issues, was a league councilor and openly supported the Mill Creek site (Winks 1997, 92). Joseph W. Ernst (1991c), a director emeritus of the Rockefeller Archive Center, points out that "until his death [in 1987], Albright served as a conservation advisor to Laurence S. Rockefeller" (2). He also explains that prior to Albright's death "correspondence flowed from Albright to Laurence S. Rockefeller as he continued and broadened his father's interests and activities in the nationwide conservation and park movement" (2). Laurence Rockefeller's biographer, Robin Winks (1997), points out that "when LSR [Laurence Rock-efeller] took over the national park mantle from his father, Albright guided him" (45). Sierra Club president Edgar Wayburn recalled that Laurance Rockefeller told him that he was going to follow Albright and Drury's advice, his "long-standing advisors," on the redwood park issue (as quoted in Cohen 1988, 308). Winks argues that the individuals that LSR "most trusted" on the redwood issue were league president Richard Leonard and Newton Drury (92).

Laurance Rockefeller played a leading role in promoting the Mill Creek site. Ultimately, he was able to convince President Johnson to support this location as the appropriate area for the redwood national park (Gould 1988, 219; Winks 1997, 92). Collier and Horowitz (1976) describe Rockefeller's role in the redwood matter in the following:

> Orchestrating the forces for the Mill Creek site within the Johnson administra-tion, among the lumber companies, California's Republican administration, and among select conservationists was Laurance Rockefeller. He earlier had made several trips to northern California to soften industry opposition to the park and had satisfied himself the Mill Creek site was a good compromise, all that could be hoped for without a long and bitter struggle. He had then a significant role in get-ting President Johnson to commit himself to the Mill Creek legislation. (394–95)

Edward Crafts, a former assistant chief of the forest service and the director of the Bureau of Outdoor Recreation, attributed Johnson's choice for the redwood park location to Rockefeller. He explained that Rockefeller "was a participant and privy to all of the things that were going on and he would deal directly with the President and Mrs. Johnson on this [redwood park issue] and was very influ-ential." Crafts added that on the issue of the park's location, "I don't think the President could have cared less" (as quoted in Schrepfer 1983, 136).

The Mill Creek location was undermined as a national park location, how-ever, when in the summer of 1966 the Miller Redwood Company initiated what Udall called "spite cutting" in the area (as quoted in Schrepfer 1983, 141). Schrepfer explains that "Miller was trying to cut as quickly as possible the only area in Mill Creek outside of Jedediah Smith worthy of national park status" (145). After Miller's actions, the Simpson, Arcata, and Georgia–Pacific companies agreed to a one-year cutting moratorium in those areas "being seri-ously considered by Congress for park status" (Schrepfer 1983, 142). The National Forest Products Association pressured Miller Redwood into sus-pending its logging operations near the Jedediah Smith Redwoods State Park (Schrepfer 1983, 142). As a result of Miller Redwood's logging activity, the league in December 1966 decided to support a two-unit national park—one unit in the Miller Creek area and the other in the Redwood Creek area.

By 1967, Laurance Rockefeller was working to broker a settlement on the redwood park issue. Collier and Horowitz (1976) describe his diplomatic effort:

In an atmosphere of almost Alexandrian intrigue, he shuttled back and forth between the various principals. It was a diplomatic offensive anticipating those his brother's adviser Henry Kissinger would later wage on a global scale. He was known to be the President's ambassador, and not surprisingly, the mood of compromise [the Mill Creek area] he represented was strongly represented in the final park legislation. (395)

Winks (1997) also documents Rockefeller's role as facilitator on the redwood issue. He explains that Laurance Rockefeller "worked steadily from behind the scenes to bring the conflicting parties—the timber companies, the environmental organizations, the government of California, and the National Park Service—to some compromise" (88). Rockefeller was ultimately successful in convincing the timber firms in the area to support the creation of a redwood national park on their lands (Schrepfer 1983, 153). He was also successful in working out a compromise among these firms and having this compromise incorporated into federal policy.

Years after Udall left office, he explained that Laurence Rockefeller was responsible for the creation of the Redwood National Park. According to Udall, Rockefeller was responsible for the creation of a national park that in Udall's opinion was limited in scope. Udall also groused that Rockefeller undercut him and the Sierra Club in their quest for a more appropriate park. Moreover, Rockefeller directly worked out the deal with high-ranking officials in the timber industry and Congress. Udall also argued that it was Rockefeller's relationship with high-level timber executives that allowed him to negotiate a settlement. According to Udall:

> This [redwood national] park was the one area where [Laurance Rockefeller] really outflanked me. From the beginning he was for the kind compromise that was finally made. I had begun by being undecided, but increasingly I realized that the Sierra Club was right in their request for a large park. I was restrained to some extent by the Bureau of the Budget, but the real problem was Laurance Rockefeller. He went behind my back to President Johnson and *worked out the compromise* [emphasis added].
>
> Laurance had close ties with the people at Weyerhaeuser [Timber Company] and prided himself on the fact that he could talk to them as one businessman to another. He prided himself on being able to go up on the Hill and reason with conservatives like Congressman Aspinal. He prided himself on his ability to get everybody to agree. Having this kind of power was very important to him, more important than aiming for what was right. (as quoted in Collier and Horowitz 1976, 396)

President Johnson signed the legislation on 2 October 1968.

The scope and content of the redwood national park were determined by the timber firms. The entire park was composed of 58,000 acres, 27,468 of which was formerly state park land. The southern park unit, which composes part of the Redwood Creek watershed, included 22,476 acres of former privately owned lands. The northern park unit contained only 5,625 acres of private land. Of the total private lands incorporated into the park only 10,876 acres were old-growth redwoods (Schrepfer 1983, 157–58). Both park units are ecologically unviable. Schrepfer explains:

> The boundaries [of the park] defied the contours of the land, passing at one point through the center of a lagoon. It was obvious almost immediately that erosion caused in part by logging above the Redwood Creek corridor . . . would threaten the Tall Trees, located precariously on a horseshoe bend in the river. (158)

Miller Redwood and Arcata lost the largest proportions of their holdings to the park. The Miller company was compensated with forest service lands elsewhere. The Arcata firm lost 60 percent of its land. This company only had limited holdings in the area, which were not of sufficient size to warrant a long-term sustainable-yield operation. Therefore, the company planned to liquidate its holdings within thirty years and then sell its cut over lands (Schrepfer 1983, 153–54). As Schrepfer explains, "A cash return from the sale of virgin timber equal to the expected profits would simply speed liquidation" (154). All of the companies that exchanged their lands for cash received payments that were above market value (Schrepfer 1983, 214 and 218). The new park would eventually cost $198 million (Schrepfer 1983, 158).

In 1978, the federal government, with the help of the league and the support of the timber firms, incorporated forty-eight thousand acres of land into the Redwood Creek park unit (Schrepfer 1983, chap. 11, 214, and 219–20). Most of this land was already clear-cut and contained only 8,990 acres of virgin redwood forest. When the area was incorporated, it was estimated that the federal government would pay at least $359 million for this land (Schrepfer 1983, 226).[3] Much of this land would not be productive for years, and, because the logging practices of the firms were generally poor (Schrepfer 1983, 199; Robbins 1997), it was questionable how commercially viable these lands would be. Writing in 1997, Winks describes Redwood National Park in the following: "Even today the park is by no means secure, and gerrymandered boundaries, insufficient size, inadequate watershed areas, and too much prior damage by logging interests have compromised the park" (85).

CONCLUSION

In all three of the preceding case studies (Yosemite, Jackson Hole, and Redwood National Park), members of the economic elite provided the political resources necessary to modify public policy. In the first and third case studies, economic elites took policy ideas advocated by intellectuals and activists and incorporated these ideas into public policy. The intellectuals of the early

Sierra Club had their proposal of Yosemite Park's transfer to the federal government converted into public policy by the Southern Pacific Railroad. It was Laurance Rockefeller and the timber industry who made both the Save-the-Redwood League and the Sierra Club's idea for a redwood national park a reality. Significantly, Laurance Rockefeller and the timber industry played this dominant role within the context of growing public awareness of wilderness and environmental issues. The second case study found economic elites mobilizing environmental interest groups to incorporate the Jackson Hole area into the national park system. Hence, all three case studies strongly suggest that the most important actors within the wilderness preservation community, with respect to public policy, are economic elites. In all three of the case studies, therefore, the policymaking process operated similarly to Domhoff's "policy-planning network" model.

Moreover, the first and third case studies suggest that environmental interest groups' connections to the corporate community and the upper class have a significant effect on their political behavior. It was observed that Warren Olney's opposition to Yosemite Park's recession contributed substantially to the Sierra Club's immobility on the issue. As noted in chapter 4, Olney was a well-connected San Francisco business attorney and a Sierra Club officer and board member. It was also observed that when the Sierra Club's board of directors was dominated by members from the business community the club was a relatively conservative organization. In contrast, as the club's board became composed largely of nonbusiness members, the club adopted what can be characterized as an aggressive stance on policy goals and means. Furthermore, the Save-the-Redwood League, an organization whose leadership is largely composed of businesspeople and that is largely dependent on wealthy benefactors, continues to be a relatively conservative environmental organization.

NOTES

1. A highway built through the state parks in the 1950s also undermined their ecological viability (Schrepfer 1983, 109–11).

2. The commission endorsed the park service's Mission 66 plan (Swain 1970, 308).

3. Winks (1997, 94) places the total cost for acquisition of the Redwood National Park land at $1.65 billion.

6

~

The Legislative Process and
the Clean Air Act of 1990

In this chapter I show that the policymaking process that produced the 1990 Clean Air Act was dominated by the very special interests that the act is expected to regulate. The act was the result of industry efforts to create uniformity in clean air regulations by having the 1990 Clean Air Act stave off and supplant air pollution regulatory regimes enacted on the state and local level. The position developed in this discussion is consistent with Cahn's (1995) argument that federal environmental regulatory policies, including federal clean air policy, serve as symbolic palliatives to a public concerned about the future of the environment. Beyond that, I demonstrate that federal air policy serves a specific political and economic function—namely, to rationalize air pollution regulations to the benefit of business interests.

CLEAN AIR POLICY BEFORE 1990

The 1970 Clean Air Act inaugurated direct federal involvement in the regulation of industrial airborne emissions, as well as the airborne emissions emitted by automobiles (Jones 1975). The 1970 act provided the federal government with wide discretion to regulate the emission of industrial pollutants and mandated a 90 percent reduction in automobile emissions. However, as described by one observer in 1989, "the Clean Air Act . . . [was] considered far-reaching, even radical when it was passed in 1970, but now [it is] regarded by many critics as crippled by concessions to special interest groups and halfhearted enforcement by the Environmental Protection Agency" (Weisskopf, 7 June 1989). For example, despite data and analysis that demonstrated that industrial production results in the emission of hundreds of discrete and harmful pollutants into the atmosphere (Shabecoff, 23 March 1989; 13 April 1989; U.S. EPA 1990, 99; 1996, 171; Gottlieb et al. 1995, 135–37; Smith 2000, chap 5), it is nevertheless the case that before 1990, the Environmental Protection Agency (EPA) had set national standards for only seven toxic or hazardous airborne pollutants: asbestos, benzene, vinyl chloride, beryllium, mercury, radionuclides, and arsenic.

The 1970 Clean Air Act mandated specific regulations for six nontoxic airborne pollutants: particulate matter, sulfur dioxide, nitrogen dioxide, volatile organic compounds, carbon monoxide, and lead. Gary Bryner (1995) explains that the regulation of these pollutants has been the "heart of air pollution regulation in the United States" (52). As table 6.1 shows, however, by 1990, of these pollutants only two, particulate matter and lead, had been significantly reduced since 1970. Nitrogen dioxide had increased above 1970 levels. The other emissions had decreased but substantial and hazardous quantities of these pollutants continued to be emitted into the atmosphere.

A major reason for the continued emission of substantial amounts of carbon monoxide, nitrogen oxide, and volatile organic compounds is the automobile. Throughout the 1980s, the federal automobile tailpipe emission standard lagged significantly behind that of California. In 1990, automobiles and trucks accounted for 30 percent of total volatile organic compounds emitted, 33 percent of nitrogen oxides, and 63 percent of carbon monoxides (U.S. EPA 1995, tables 3–1, 3–2, and 3–3). Automobile emissions contributed significantly to record smog levels in 1987 and a higher ozone level in 1988 than in 1983 when

Table 6.1   Nontoxic Air Pollutants, 1970–1990

Pollutant	*1970*	*1980*	*1990*
Particulate Matter*	13	7	3.7
Sulfur Dioxide	31.2	25.9	22.4
Nitrogen Dioxide	20.6	23.2	23
VOC	30.6	25.9	23.6
CO	128	115.6	100.7
Lead	219.5	75	5.7

Notes: Except for lead, all figures in million short tons. Lead is in one thousand short tons. (One short ton equals two thousand pounds.) VOC = volatile organic compounds; CO = carbon monoxide.

*The 1990 data for particulate matter does not include fugitive dust emissions. The EPA began collecting data for fugitive dust emissions in 1985.

Source: Environmental Protection Agency. 1996 October. *National Air Pollutant Emission Trends, 1900–1995*, 14–15. Research Triangle Park, N.C.: Office of Air Quality Planning and Standards.

the previous record was set. Furthermore, in 1988, twenty-eight additional cities, counties, and other areas were exceeding ozone EPA standards above the prior year. This brought the total number of areas that exceeded ozone standards to one hundred (Shabecoff, 1 March 1989). According to the EPA, by 1989 automobiles accounted for 45 percent of hydrocarbons, a volatile organic material, emitted in urban areas (U.S. Congress 1990b, 232). When acted on by sunlight, hydrocarbons and nitrogen oxides together produce ozone, which can cause severe respiratory problems.[1] In addition, ozone at low atmospheric levels, when mixed with dust and other particulate matter, becomes smog.

STATE AND LOCAL AIR POLLUTION POLICIES

In response to the moderate efforts of the federal government, many states and localities in the 1980s began to initiate their own air pollution regulations. These developments led the chemical industry to hold a conference in 1989 in Washington, D.C., on the issue of state and local regulations. Geoffrey Hurwitz, director of state government relations for Rohm and Haas Co., a Philadelphia-based chemical company, argued at the conference that the various state and local regulations were creating "a legal balkanization threat that, in the environmental arena, we ignore at our peril" (as quoted in Kriz, 9 December 1989, 2989). Several local jurisdictions, for example, had established their own regulations on the composition of house paint and lacquer to reduce air pollution (Wald, 10 October 1989). Later in an interview, Hurwitz stated, "I'm arguing for a more assertive federal government in terms of preemption issues and having the guts to say that in certain areas, it makes sense to have national environmental laws" (as quoted in Kriz, 9 December 1989, 2990). As a result of increasing state and local regulations, William P. Buckley, state and local government relations manager for Eastman Kodak, exhorted chemical firms at the Washington conference to increase their political activity in trendsetting states, such as California, New York, and Florida, even if they did not have facilities in these states (Kriz, 9 December 1989, 2990).

Furthermore, in the late 1980s certain states began to impose stricter standards on automobile emissions than those set by the federal government. California under federal law is allowed to establish its own automobile emission standards. Federal law also allows states to adopt either the federal or California standards (Ridge 1994, 175–77). In the summer of 1989, the governors of New York, New Jersey, and the six New England states announced that their states planned to adopt the stricter California standards (Lowry 1992, chap. 4).

In response to the action by the northeastern states, General Motors argued that "if auto manufacturers are forced to respond to a patchwork of different emissions standards throughout the nation production, distribution and sales of vehicles will become increasingly complex and costly to customers" (as quoted in Wald, 11 August 1989). An aide to Representative Henry Waxman

(D-Calif.), the chair of the House Health and Environment Subcommittee and a friend of environmentalists, pointed out that the prospective adoption of the California standards by the northeastern states "had a big impact on Congress." The aide went on to argue:

> California and the northeastern states are 20–30 percent of the auto market. Once they [the northeastern states] went forward, it made it a lot easier to set the [California] standard on the federal level because industry's going to have to meet the requirements in the other states anyway. (as quoted in Kriz, 9 December 1989, 2989)

Complicating matters further for the automobile industry, in September 1989, California announced that it planned to adopt a plan that would mandate the additional reduction of automobile emissions (Matthews, 29 September 1990). This plan, which went into effect in September 1990, would further complicate matters from a legal perspective and for the automobile industry. Would the automobile industry now have three different emission standards to meet? Or would those states that adopted the old California emission standards now have to adopt the new California standards? Furthermore, if the northeastern states are allowed to set automobile emission standards that are different from the federal government or California, will this allow other states to establish their own unique standards?

Three days after California announced its new emission standard, Representatives John Dingell (D-Mich.) and Waxman reached an agreement to make the old California emission standards part of the House version of the 1990 Clean Air Act (Hager, 7 October 1989). This agreement paved the way for the old California standards to be incorporated into the final legislation. Additionally, a "no-third vehicle" clause was incorporated into the 1990 Clean Air Act (42 U.S.C. section 7507 [Supp. IV 1992]). Legal scholar John Ridge (1994) explains that this aspect of the act prevents "the states from adopting new tailpipe emissions standards which cause or have the effect of causing the [automobile] manufacturers to have to create a new vehicle or engine" apart from those prompted by the federal and California emission standards (176).

States also began in the late 1980s to consider gasoline and its reformulation, or its possible replacement, as a potential means to reduce air pollution. The northeastern states that adopted the California automobile emission standards also set standards concerning the formulation of gasoline. Specifically, in 1989 these states required that gasoline volatility be reduced from a Reid vapor pressure of 11.5, which was voluntarily set by the oil industry, to one of nine. The Reid vapor pressure scale is how gasoline volatility is measured. California had already mandated a Reid vapor pressure of nine. Greater gasoline volatility makes it easier for an automobile to start in cold weather; greater gasoline volatility, however, also increases the amount of smog-creating pollution that an automobile emits. The oil industry opposed the northeastern regulation on gasoline because the reduction of Reid pressure requires the reduction of butane, which inexpensively adds volume to gasoline. In addition, butane increases the level of octane in gasoline, and as a result of oil company marketing campaigns, customers have developed a preference for high-octane gasoline (Wald, 6 March 1989).

According to the Clean Air Act of 1970, the EPA was supposed to set a national Reid vapor pressure standard, but it had failed to do so. This failure allowed the states to set their own standard. In response to the initiative on the part of the northeastern states, the EPA promulgated a Reid vapor pressure of 10.5 to 9.5, which was supposed to supplant the northeastern states' Reid vapor pressure standard. Massachusetts, however, threatened to sue, and the EPA allowed the states' stricter rule to stand (Wald, 25 March 1989).

The oil industry opposed the standard set by the states and supported the new EPA standard. The oil industry trade organization, the American Petroleum Institute, sued unsuccessfully in New York courts to prevent the implementation of the northeastern states' rule (Wald, 10 October 1989). In contrast, the Institute praised the new less restrictive volatility standard set by the EPA (Shabecoff, 11 March 1989).

In addition to the actions of the northeast, Colorado in 1987 began a program that mandated that gasoline sold during the winter months contain oxygenated additives ("Colorado's High-Oxygen Fuel Test Runs Smoothly," 1 March 1988). The addition of oxygenated additives, such as ethanol or methyl tertiary butyl ether (MTBE), reduces the amount of smog-producing chemicals created when gasoline is burned. Furthermore, prior to 1990, programs in Washington State, California, New York City, and British Columbia began experimenting with alternative-fuel vehicles (Wald, 7 April 1989).

From the oil industry's perspective, both alternative fuels and gasoline additives are problematic solutions to automobile emissions. Alternative fuels, such as methanol, electricity, or natural gas, which can be substantially less polluting than conventional gasoline, represent a threat to the oil industry's lucrative gasoline market. Automobiles, however, have already begun to reach the limits of emissions reduction while burning conventional gasoline. Automobiles by 1989 had reduced the emission of hydrocarbons by 80 percent and nitrogen oxides by 60 percent, when compared to automobiles produced in the 1960s (U.S. Congress 1990b, 227).[2] In congressional testimony, William G. Rosenberg, assistant administrator for air and radiation for the EPA, stated that, short of restricting the use of automobiles, a substitution of alternative fuels for conventional gasoline would be the only means through which to achieve ozone attainment standards in several urban areas (U.S. Congress 1990b, 227–28).

Fuel additives, while used with gasoline, do represent a production problem for the oil industry. Because oil-based fuels, such as gasoline, jet fuel, heating oil, and heavy fuel oil, are all produced from the same barrel of oil and in the same production process, adding an additive to gasoline results in complications in producing other oil-based fuels. Specifically, generally half of a refined barrel of oil becomes gasoline and the other half becomes other forms of fuels, and very little can be done to alter this (Lippman, 12 June 1990). Hence, a reduction in the production of gasoline to make room for a substantial amount of additive will result in a corresponding reduction in other fuels. Conversely, to refine more oil to produce greater amounts of other fuels would increase the amount of gasoline beyond market demand.

Given these factors, it is simpler to develop and apply technologies to automobiles, such as catalytic converters, to reduce car emissions than it is to modify gasoline to achieve reductions because automotive technologies tend to only affect cost that can be passed on to customers. From the perspective of maintaining clean air, focusing on automobiles, as opposed to gasoline, to lower automotive emissions, is not the optimal solution. First, it takes several years for new low-emission models to supplant older, higher-emission models in the automotive population, whereas the introduction of cleaner fuels immediately reduces emissions from all automobiles. This occurred, for example, with the distribution and sale of unleaded gasoline. Second, the older an automobile becomes, the more it pollutes regardless of antipollution innovations.

With respect to the formulation of the 1990 Clean Air Act, the oil industry lobbied to have gasoline emission standards set within the law, rather than have the law set specific gasoline contents. It argued that this would allow the oil and automobile industries to work together to meet gasoline combustion emission standards.[3] The oil industry also argued that if gasoline contents were not set within legislation, it would have the flexibility to meet the law's emission standards with a minimum amount of disruption to the fuel production process (U.S. Congress 1990a, 71; 1990b, 368; Lippman, 12 June 1990). Michael E. Canes, vice president of policy for the American Petroleum Institute, argued in congressional testimony:

> Efforts to set specifications for reformulated gasoline are premature and should be avoided. . . . Instead, air quality performance standards should be set for the fuel vehicle system[,] and auto manufacturers and fuel suppliers should be allowed to develop the most efficient means of meeting these standards. (U.S. Congress 1990a, 71)

With increasing regulations instituted on the local and state level, industry in the late 1980s turned to the federal government to have it reassert its role in the area of air pollution policy. This reassertion would work to take the initiative away from state and local actors who would otherwise each seek to impose their own regulations on industry.

The Issue Network Involved in the 1990 Clean Air Act Policymaking Process

Several organizations designed to mediate and reconcile business policy preferences on the issue of clean air were active in the 1990 Clean Air Act policymaking process. There were the traditional trade organizations: the American Petroleum Institute, the Motor Vehicle Manufacturers Association, the Edison Electric Institute, the Chemical Manufacturers Association, and the National Coal Association. Also active on the issue of clean air were the National Association of Manufacturers and the U.S. Chamber of Commerce, both of which are composed of businesses from several corporate sectors ("People: Air Forces," 21 April 1990). Furthermore, the Business Roundtable, an organization composed of the chief executive officers of the largest two hundred firms in the United States, was also active in the policymaking process of the 1990 Clean Air Act. All of these organizations can potentially serve as a means for the business community to develop a consensus on public policy and then have their resources directed at the implementation of the agreed-on policy.

In addition to the aforementioned long-standing business organizations, the corporate community also created the Clean Air Working Group (CAWG) to deal specifically with air pollution policy. The CAWG is an umbrella organization encompassing all those industrial sectors that would presumably be affected directly by proposed clean air legislation. According to an internal CAWG document:[4]

> The Clean Air Working Group is composed of more than 100 representatives of the business and industrial community in Washington who are concerned with the Clean Air Act. The industries represented, by either company or trade association people, are agriculture, aluminum, automotive, automotive parts, chemicals, coal, construction equipment, containers, contractors, drugs, electric utilities, farm equipment, fiberglass, food products, forest products, glass, heavy mobile equipment, mining, paints and coatings, paper, petroleum, railroads, realtors, rubber, service industries, steel, wholesalers, and a variety of manufacturing companies. In addition, several organizations representing business and industry generally are included in the group. (Clean Air Working Group 1981a)

Among CAWG's members are the Chemical Manufacturers Association, DuPont, the Edison Electric Institute, Ford, General Motors, the National Association of Manufacturers, the National Coal Association, the American Petroleum Institute, and the Motor Vehicles Manufacturers Association (Adler 1992, 27).

As reported by George Hager (20 January 1990) of the *Congressional Quarterly Weekly*, the CAWG was not only a lobbying organization for businesses concerned with environmental legislation; it also served as a mechanism for business groups to resolve disputes among themselves and to present the consensus proposals to the administration and Congress (Cohen 1995, 125):

> Living down its no-bill image is not CAWG's only problem. Just as tough is trying to reach consensus among industries with competing clean-air goals, or even within industries that are at war with themselves.
>
> [William] Fay [the CAWG's administrator] says CAWG's goal is to resolve disputes [between and within industrial sectors] and avoid repeating the mistakes industry made the last time Congress revamped clean-air laws, when some industries cut separate deals to exempt themselves for tight new controls. That allowed legislators to form an environmental coalition that had the votes to pass the 1977 amendments to the Clean Air Act.
>
> Never again, Fay says. With the CAWG rule, he says, "you've got to work your issues, but you have to stick with the group even after you may get your amendments." (147)

Hence, Fay reports that CAWG industry members were expected to continue lobbying on environmental legislation on behalf of other corporate sectors even when their own issues were resolved. In this respect the CAWG is best viewed as an institution dedicated to the development of an acceptable clean air policy for American industry as a class.

As early as 1981, when it began meeting on a weekly basis (Cohen 1995, 124–25), the CAWG had developed policy proposals on twelve specific clean air issues: (1) national ambient air quality standards, (2) prevention of significant deterioration, (3) nonattainment requirements, (4) control technology requirements, (5) procedures for revision of state implementation plans and issuance of permits, (6) acid rains, (7) hazardous air pollutants, (8) visibility, (9) new source performance standards, (10) noncompliance penalties, (11) mobile sources, and (12) judicial review (Clean Air Working Group 1981b). To develop its expertise and to formulate specific policy proposals, the CAWG divided its "operations into roughly 10 separate teams handling the key clean-air issues" (Cohen 1995, 125). Cohen goes on to report that the CAWG's "weekly meetings, usually attended by more than 100 corporate lobbyists, often featured freewheeling discussions among different industry groups" (125–26). Therefore, as the need arose in the late 1980s to revise the Clean Air Act, the CAWG had developed the knowledge and expertise to produce policy proposals that were technically sound.

Overall, industry in 1989 came out in support for new amendments to the Clean Air Act. The CAWG's public stance was that it, and its constituent members, would support new clean air legislation that increased environmental regulation as long as the legislation was rational and affordable. Particularly significant was the support expressed by both the oil and chemical industries for the idea of new clean air legislation (Hager, 20 January 1990).

The environmental lobby also centralized its lobbying efforts. The National

Clean Air Coalition (NCAC) is an umbrella organization composed of public service groups concerned with clean air. It is made up of virtually all major environmental groups, as well as church groups, civic and public health groups, and labor unions (Weisskopf, 19 April 1990; Adler 1992, 25; Cohen 1995, 117–18). This organization took the lead for the environmental community on the issue of clean air (Hager, 20 January 1990). Its chairman was Richard Ayres.

Other environmental organizations active in the clean air policymaking process were the Sierra Club, the Environmental Defense Fund, the Izaak Walton League, Environmental Action Inc., and the National Wildlife Federation. Non-environmental public interest groups were also active, specifically the American Lung Association and the United States Public Interest Research Group, an environmental and consumer advocacy organization. The United Steel Workers also took an active interest in the clean air legislation being developed ("People," 14 April 1990). Finally, the state environmental agencies from California and New York were involved in the clean air policymaking process.

Therefore, the network surrounding the 1990 Clean Air Act was sufficiently developed enough to qualify for what Heclo (1978) considers to be a democratically configured "issue network." In other words, while the clean air issue network contained powerful business interests, it was also composed of groups and individuals believed to be concerned largely with the public interest. According to Heclo (1978) and Skocpol (1992), the substantial presence of groups and individuals concerned with the public interest should have allowed government officials to draw upon their ideas and political energy in determining the shape and content of the 1990 Clean Air Act.

Consequently, if the pluralist or state autonomy/issue network models represent an accurate depiction of the policymaking process, the final legislative result should represent a meaningful compromise between the views of these competing organizations. If, however, the plural elite and economic elite positions are more accurate, one should find that the final legislative result closely resembled the position of business and that the environmental groups' proposals were generally defeated.

CLEAN AIR ACT OF 1990: THE POLICYMAKING PROCESS

Acid Rain

Within the Bush administration, a "tribunal" was responsible for the formulation of the president's clean air legislation. This group was headed by President Bush's chief of staff, John Sununu. Its other members were William Reilly, head of the EPA; Richard G. Darman, director of the Office of Management and Budget; and Energy Secretary James D. Watkins. Among this group only Reilly, former head of the Environmental Defense Fund and the Conservation Fund, could be considered a champion of the environment. The others could be characterized as conservatives primarily sympathetic to business and its perspective and preferences (Weisskopf, 30 July 1989).

One of the provisions of the Bush bill, and ultimately of the final legislation, was directly attributed to an environmental group—the Environmental Defense Fund (EDF) (Title IV). The EDF is credited with directly crafting that portion of the legislation that provides for a permit trading system that is expected to induce the reduction of emissions from power plants in the Midwest and Appalachia (Schneider, 28 October 1990; Cohen 1995, 61–66; Ellerman et al. 2000, chap. 2). Under this system, polluters who reduce their emissions below a prescribed amount can sell permits or "allowances" that equal the total of their excess reduction to other power plants that are above the set limit. In turn, firms that exceed their emission limit must purchase permits from those firms that have reduced their emissions below government standards.

This permit trading system is expected to help internalize the cost of pollution and hence give firms an economic incentive to reduce emissions. Furthermore, for those firms that reduce their emissions below government limits, the trading system is expected to financially reward them for continuing to reduce emissions. The objective of this system is to reduce the emission of sulfur dioxide from power plants by ten million tons from 1980 levels by 2010 (Weisskopf, 30 July 1989; 22 October 1990; Bryner 1997, 92–93; Ellerman et al. 2000).

As argued by Bryner (1997), however, permit trading systems are a second-best means to internalize the costs of pollution. The optimal method to internalize the costs of pollution is to tax directly the amount of pollution produced or the material that produces a particular pollutant.[5] Additionally, Hahn and Hester's study, published in 1989, found that programs designed to promote the reduction of ambient emissions through permit trading systems had neither induced active interfirm permit trading nor had significantly improved air quality. Hahn and Hester (1989) did find that permit trading systems had reduced costs for firms.[6]

A significant flaw of the acid rain portion of the 1990 Clean Air Act is that it does not prohibit the usage of high-sulfur coal and mandate the utilization of low-sulfur coal. The burning of high-sulfur coal by power plants located in the Midwest and Appalachia results in the emission of substantial amounts of sulfur dioxide. This emission of sulfur dioxide in turn produces acid rain that falls largely in the Northeast and Canada. Low-sulfur coal, a viable substitute for high-sulfur coal, is a low-tech and inexpensive means through which to reduce sulfur dioxide emissions from power plants. Moreover, the mandated usage of low-sulfur coal does not necessitate a significant government presence to assess compliance. In contrast, the permit trading system enacted in the 1990 Clean Air Act does require assiduous monitoring (Braadbaart 1998; Weber 1998, 160–64). Significantly, since the passage of the 1990 Clean Air Act, government agencies have not sufficiently increased the number officials devoted to monitoring compliance with the acid rain regulatory regime (Weber 1998, 173).

Ackerman and Hassler (1981) contend that the 1977 amendments to the Clean Air Act did not mandate the usage of low-sulfur coal to reduce emissions from high-sulfur coal power plants because the states where these power plants are located have large reserves of high-sulfur coal. Hence, Congress did not prohibit the use of high-sulfur coal in 1977, because, in substantial part, of the political clout of the coal interests in those states. Instead of restricting the utilization of high-sulfur coal, Congress in the 1977 Clean Air Act required the utilization of the best available technology (i.e., scrubbers) to reduce sulfur dioxide emissions from power plants in the Midwest and Appalachia.[7]

Automobile and Fuel Emission Standards

The key provisions in the 1990 Clean Air Act concerning automobile and fuel emissions were formulated in the House of Representatives—specifically, in the House Energy and Commerce Committee.[8] The chairperson of this committee was Democrat John Dingell of Michigan, who is widely considered to be a close ally of the automobile industry (Kriz, 23 September 1989; Hook, 12 May 1990, 1453; Melnick 1992, 89; Cohen 1995, 3). Dingell sponsored the administration's bill in the House. With respect to the policymaking process within the House, a coalition within the Energy and Commerce Committee, led by Dingell, governed this process (Cohen 1995, 132). With the exception of one issue, Dingell's coalition held together throughout the entire mark-up process within the committee and its Subcommittee on Health and Environment.

The House Health and Environment Subcommittee was responsible for writing the clean air legislation for presentation to the full committee on Energy and Commerce. In this subcommittee, chaired by Waxman, an alliance consistently defeated amendments proposed by the liberals and environmentalists in the subcommittee. Hager (30 September 1989) notes the general dynamic of the ideological voting blocs in the subcommittee:

> [Henry] Waxman's [(D-Calif.)] decision to let his proposal die without a roll-call vote was another sign that the panel [the House Health and Environment Subcommittee] was moving against him—and toward the White House proposal—on crucial issues.
>
> [John] Dingell [(D-Mich.)] and [Norman] Lent [(R-N.Y.)] have generally managed to hold a solid bloc of Republicans and moderate-to-conservative Democrats behind their substitute version of the Bush package. Environmentalists and their House allies expect that trend to continue when the bill moves to the full committee. (2552)

The Democrats on the subcommittee, who consistently voted against Waxman's initiatives, were referred to as the "group of nine." Hager (23 September 1989) writes, "The moderate-to-conservative Democrats known as the 'group of nine'

... have formed a potent, swing-vote opposition to the Waxman faction" (2451). Christopher Madison (7 October 1989), a journalist for the *National Journal,* who also covered the 1990 Clean Air Act policymaking process, points out:

> Dingell . . . joined forces with the [Energy and Commerce] committee's ranking Republican, Norman F. Lent of New York, to sponsor a package of modifications that became the basis for the Waxman subcommittee markup. The result of this maneuvering has been a middle-of-the-road, bipartisan coalition controlled by Dingell.

Michael Weisskopf (10 October 1989), who covered the 1990 Clean Air Act policymaking process for the *Washington Post,* labeled the coalition that dominated the subcommittee an "auto-oil bloc."

It was in this subcommittee that California emission standards were written into the clean air legislation (Title II). The standards were adopted by a vote of 22–0. In addition to establishing California emission standards as the national standards, Waxman proposed that the clean air legislation mandate a second round of emission reductions that would have automatically been implemented in 2000. Richard Ayres declared in congressional testimony that "we wish to express strong support especially for the second round of tailpipe standards" (U.S. Congress 1990a, 67). Also, Tom Jorling, the commissioner of the New York State Department of Environmental Conservation, and Tom Cackette, the deputy executive officer of the California Air Resources Board, both expressed in congressional testimony their strong support for a mandatory second round of tailpipe emission reductions (U.S. Congress 1990a, 36 and 38). In contrast, the proposed second round of emission reductions was adamantly opposed by the automobile industry. Donald R. Buist, director of automotive emissions and fuel economy for the Ford Motor Co., stated in congressional testimony, "The retention of second tier tailpipe standards continues to concern us. Manufacturers have testified, and government experts agree, that there is no present technology, nor do they know when technology would be available to achieve the second tier levels" (U.S. Congress 1990a, 52).

Instead of an automatic second round of emission reductions, the final legislation included language that made it much less likely that a second round of reductions would ever be implemented. Specifically, the 1990 Clean Air Act calls on the EPA in 2003 to 2006 to study the need for further automobile emission reductions. After such a study, according to the act, the EPA can either reaffirm the existing standards or set new stricter standards. If the EPA does neither, stricter standards automatically go into effect (Hager, 7 October 1989).

The House Health and Environment Subcommittee also eliminated an amendment proposed by the Bush administration that would have mandated that automakers produce one million alternative fuel cars annually by 1997.[9] The provision was strongly promoted by leaders of the environmental community. In congressional testimony, Richard Ayres, chairperson of the National Clean Air Coalition, declared that the automobile emission "reductions promised in the President's clean fuels proposal should serve as the minimum cleanup objective for an alternative fuels program" (U.S. Congress 1990a, 67). Also, both Jorling and Cackette in congressional testimony expressed support for the use of alternative fuels in fighting air pollution. Cackette, for example, stated before the Senate Subcommittee on Environmental Protection, "We . . . believe that the severe and extreme nonattainment areas of the country will need the additional [automobile] emission reductions from alternative fuels or clean fuels, and that these reductions can be achieved most effectively using these alternative fuels" (U.S. Congress 1990a, 39). The Bush administration did not fight for its alternative fuel amendment (Weisskopf, 10 October 1989; 12 October 1989; Hager, 14 October 1989; Cohen 1995, 154). Instead of mandating the production of alternative fuel automobiles, the House version, and ultimately the final legislation, required that automobile companies be able only to demonstrate that they are capable of the production and distribution of alternative fuel automobiles (Cohen 1995, 159). Richard Ayres rejected this substitute approach to alternative fuels, embodied in the Halls–Fields Amendment, as a "sham" (U.S. Congress 1990a, 67).

The House subcommittee also drafted the final legislation's language on reformulated gasoline (Title II). The key aspects of this provision were crafted by the oil industry (Babcock and Weisskopf, 22 May 1990; Wald, 25 September 1990).[10] It calls for the sale of so-called clean gasoline in the nine most polluted cities: Los Angeles, Houston, New York, Baltimore, Chicago, Milwaukee, Philadelphia, San Diego, and most of Connecticut.[11] The legislation set gasoline emission standards for the gasoline sold in these nine areas, but the oil industry would determine how to meet these standards (Weisskopf, 22 October 1990; Adler 1992, 36; Cohen 1995, 167–68).[12]

Hence, with the exception of a pilot program in California, the final bill did not mandate the imposition of alternative fuels or fuel additives in gasoline that would assuredly reduce smog producing chemicals.[13] Daniel Weiss, director of the Sierra Club's pollution program, complained that unless the government set specific fuel content requirements, the new "clean" fuels promulgated by oil companies could be gimmicks or public relation ploys. He specifically alleged that "it's important to note that many of these so-called reformulated gasolines still have the same content" (as quoted in Kriz, 2 June 1990, 1330–31).

Richard Ayres of the National Clean Air Coalition was particularly critical of the provisions of the act that dealt with automobile emissions and urban smog. He argued that "with respect to urban smog, the bill provides too long for too many to do too little" (as quoted in Cohen, 27 October 1990). Ayres also remarked that the 1990 Clean Air Act automobile emission "requirements will certainly give us cleaner urban air, but they don't seem strong enough to give us healthful air under Federal standards" (as quoted in Gold, 30 October 1990). In addition, Albert F. Appleton, New York City environmental commissioner, stated, "New York City's worst air problem is caused by automobiles and the bottom line of the [1990] Clean Air Act is: automobiles, one: clean air, nothing" (as quoted in Schneider, 23 October 1990).

Dingell's coalition divided on one issue. The president's bill would have allowed automobile manufacturers to meet emission standards through the averaging of fleet emissions, as opposed to imposing regulations on each individual automobile. The Bush provision was supported by Dingell and opposed by environmentalists. The provision was expunged from the legislation. This was the single defeat for Dingell's coalition. He later argued that the EPA could change the administrative rules governing how cars meet federal emission standards without the approval of Congress (Weisskopf, 21 September 1989; Hager, 23 September 1989, 2452).

Finally, as a result of the composition of the committee and subcommittee responsible for writing the clean air legislation for the House, the House bill for the most part ignored the policy preferences of environmentalists. This is particularly the case with the central issues of automobile and fuel emissions. The committee bill passed in the full House with a 401–21 vote, without any contentious floor amendments.

Events in the Senate

On the Senate side, this congressional chamber approved a clean air bill that was very similar to that of the House. The route through the Senate, however, was more laborious and circuitous. Its difficulties originated in the fact that the Senate committee (the Environment and Public Works Committee) and subcommittee (the Subcommittee on Environmental Protection) entrusted with marking up clean air legislation produced strong regulatory legislation (Cohen 1995, 86–89). The Senate committee and subcommittee produced a bill that in many respects far outdid the Bush administration proposals in protecting the environment. On a 10–0 vote, for example, the Senate subcommittee passed an amendment on urban smog that

> Senate committee members and staff say . . . is much tougher than Bush's bill in how it spells out compliance methods, in how it would limit the discretion of the Environmental Protection Agency in guiding cities toward compliance, and how it would penalize cities that fail to meet their initial compliance goals. (Hager, 28 October 1989, 2864)

The committee bill also contained a mandatory second round of motor vehicle emission reductions. Overall, the Senate committee produced legislation that, "while similar in structure to a Bush Administration clean-air package . . . the

Senate bill goes beyond Bush's bill in many areas, calling for more certain pollution reduction, tougher restrictions on industry and tighter controls on motor vehicles" (Hager, 18 November 1990, 3145).

Richard Ayres expressed cautious approval of the Senate legislation, considering it "basically a sound bill" (as quoted in Hager, 28 October 1989, 2864). Later he commented that he was happy with the final legislation produced by the Senate committee and that many of the difficulties that he saw in the Senate bill were "details at this point" (as quoted in Hager, 18 November 1990, 3145). Remarking on the events in the Senate committee, the Sierra Club Washington representative, Blake Early, lauded them for adding "some much-needed strengthening amendments to the bill" (as quoted in Hager, 21 October 1989, 2784).

Not only did the committee go beyond the Bush administration's proposals for the legislation, but it also was apparently at odds with business policy preferences. William Fay denounced the bill produced in the Senate subcommittee as "too extreme for the degree of the problem" (as quoted in Hager, 28 October 1989). The Business Roundtable based its opposition to the Senate committee's legislation on a study it produced that found that the proposed legislation would cost what it felt would be the exorbitant amount of $104 billion annually (Kriz, 27 January 1990). The Ford Motor Co. argued that the bill reported out of the Senate committee placed impossible technological requirements on the automobile industry and "unnecessarily high costs for minimal air quality benefits" (as quoted in Hager, 18 November 1989, 3145).

The committee's legislation did not have enough support in the Senate to avoid a threatened filibuster (Hager, 10 February 1990, 386; Cohen 1995, 86–89 and 93–94). As a result, White House and Senate negotiators went behind closed doors to work out a compromise (Cohen 1995, 92–95). The bill that emerged from these closed-door meetings angered environmentalists and in turn came much closer to business preferences on clean air legislation:

> [Richard] Ayres [chairman of the National Clean Air Coalition] and others charged that the negotiators had retreated across the board, and they insisted that, in some respects, the substitute would weaken existing law. They vowed to oppose it.
>
> Industry representatives, in contrast, were relieved to see the bill go into closed-door talks and happier with what came out than what went in. "The movement's in the right direction," said Bill Fay, administrator of the industry-funded Clean Air Working Group. (Hager, 3 March 1990, 654)

Also, Gene Karpinski, director of the United States Public Interest Research Group, an environmental and consumer advocacy organization, said of the Senate–White House compromise bill that "the clean air bill went into the back rooms and it looks like a dirty air bill is coming out" (as quoted in Shabecoff, 2 March 1990). In response to the critical comments made by environmentalists of the compromise bill, Senator George Mitchell (D-Me.), who was the chief Senate negotiator, remarked that environmentalist lobbyists "were not helpful" and that "they spent most of their time attacking their friends" in the Senate (as quoted in "People," 14 April 1990). Furthermore, Richard Cohen (1995) reports that the environmental lobby's "opposition to his efforts [to develop and enact a compromise bill] produced for [Senator] Mitchell what he called 'the most difficult aspect' of the debate" surrounding the 1990 Clean Air Act (99).

In the end, despite the pro-environmental stance of the Senate committee charged with writing the clean air legislation, the Senate bill was very similar to that passed by the House, where industry allies were in greater control of the legislative process.[14] As pointed out by the *Congressional Quarterly Weekly*, "Although there are hundreds of differences between the 507-page House measure and its 698-page Senate counterpart, many of them significant, the two bills are so alike in general philosophy and overall structure that participants expect no intractable disputes when negotiators meet in conference" (Hager, 26 May 1990, 1643). Specifically, the White House–Senate bill did not contain a mandatory second round of automobile emission reductions, it significantly weakened the toxic emission provisions of the original Senate committee bill, and the compromise bill weakened regulatory controls proposed for the industrial emission of hydrocarbons (Weisskopf, 7 February 1990; 1 March 1990; 2 March 1990). The compromise bill passed the Senate by a vote of 89–11.

With the death of the Senate committee bill, the one source of environmental groups' access to the policymaking process was shut off. Reflective of this, Richard Cohen (1995), who offers a detailed description of the events in the White House and Congress surrounding the formulation and enactment of the 1990 Clean Air Act, writes that "by 1990, when the clean-air bill was at the top of the agenda for Washington power brokers, the environmentalists had been pushed toward the sidelines" (122). It is this lack of meaningful access that prompted most of the negative comments made by environmental lobbyists documented throughout this discussion.

In contrast, corporate lobbyists were generally positive toward the final legislation. While Fay of the Clean Air Working Group remained consistent with business's antiregulatory and antistate public image by grousing that the 1990 Clean Air Act "could've been written more affordably," he went on to say that "we're not going to fight it" (as quoted in Weisskopf, 28 October 1990). Other industry lobbyists were more positive toward the final legislation. For example, "As conferees prepared to ratify their agreement [of] Oct. 22 [1990], Ron Sykes of General Motors Corp. handed a cigar to Bill Becker, a lobbyist for state and local pollution control officials, who had pushed for tough new pollution control standards" (Pytte, 27 October 1990, 3588). In addition, officials from both DuPont and the Motor Vehicle Manufacturers Association expressed support and contentment with the final legislation (Schneider, 23 October 1990). Also, a

New York Times reporter, Keith Schneider (28 October 1990), conveyed the following incident after Congress approved the final clean air legislation: "In the halls of the Rayburn House Office Building, lobbyists for oil, auto, chemical and utility companies put down their cellular phones and celebrated the end of weeks of wearying negotiations with handshakes and backslaps." Schneider went on to report that "some environmentalists complain that the reason industry is embracing the bill is because of a host of exemptions and overly generous timetables."

PLURAL ELITE/ECONOMIC ELITE THEORY AND CLEAN AIR POLICY

The 1990 Clean Air Act benefited the business community by rationalizing environmental regulations under largely one national regulatory regime.[15] Moreover, in responding to the business community's objections, those officials directly responsible for determining the content of the 1990 Clean Air Act prevented environmental activists from participating meaningfully in the formulation process that produced the act. The most significant environmentalist proposal to make it into the act—the permit trading system—conforms to the corporate view of a regulatory regime. Specifically, it relies on market incentives and does not utilize pollution taxes, nor does it emphasize command-and-control regulatory techniques, such as a prohibition against high-sulfur coal.[16] As a result of the limited role of environmental activists in this policymaking process, the national regulatory regime established under the 1990 Clean Air Act reflected strongly the policy preferences of those segments of the corporate community affected by the new regulatory regime. This is especially evident in those aspects of the legislation that deal with automobile and fuel emissions.

Furthermore, the limited role of environmental activists in the policy formulation process has significant implications for state theory. This limited role tends to support both the plural elite and the economic elite theory claims about the distribution of political power. Moreover, the political behavior of the business community and its ability to seemingly dominate such a broad policy area as clean air provides additional support for the economic elite model of policymaking and business political behavior.

CLEAN AIR POLICY: PLURALISM OR CORPORATE LIBERALISM?

One can argue that the development of U.S. clean air policy is consistent with pluralism. Despite the fact that this policy regime has been historically weak and that the most substantial expansion of clean air regulatory policies was largely shaped by the corporate community, the ultimate preference of this community is to *not* have any regulatory policy whatsoever. Therefore, with

Chapter 6

one set of interest groups desiring no regulatory policies and a competing group (i.e., environmentalists) demanding strong regulatory policies, a weak policy regime could be viewed as the type of compromise consistent with pluralism.

This, however, is only at first glance. A detailed analysis would find that corporate liberalism is a more accurate assessment of U.S. clean air policy, and it is more consistent with the policymaking process described earlier. Proponents of corporate liberalism argue that it is a political perspective within the business community. Specifically, according to its advocates, corporate liberals are willing to accept, and will even advocate, mild reforms of capitalism in exchange for social and political stability (Weinstein 1968; Eakins 1972). Eakins, in the following, describes the perspective and the political activity of those within the corporate community who donned the corporate liberal view during the Progressive era:

> The corporate liberal . . . was a reformer who was motivated by a fairly rational fear of the socialist appeal; by his own immediate interest in stability and profits; and by his understanding that the long-range stability of the capitalist structure could only be ensured through a national corporate political-economic responsibility. And he was brought to this position by outside demands. Thus it was that the corporate liberal came to advocate many of the same reforms proposed by political liberals. (191)

Eakins goes on to point out, however, that "it was the corporate liberal who dominated and defined twentieth-century reform" (191–92). Therefore, according to the corporate liberal perspective, economic logic is not the only factor motivating and guiding business political behavior, but this behavior is influenced in many instances by political and social factors.

The development of U.S. clean air policy is consistent with the corporate liberal model. For example, despite the fact that automobile manufacturers were a major target of the 1970 Clean Air Act, they put up only token opposition against it (Jones 1975; Vogel 1989). Corporate liberalism could help explain why despite the fact that a conservative mood prevailed in Washington, D.C., during the early and mid-1980s, the federal government did not eviscerate existing environmental legislation (Kraft 1994, 1997). In addition, in the late 1980s when local and state air pollution regulations began to hamper the operation of the national economy, the corporate community did not try to eliminate these state and local regulations. Instead, this community rationalized the nation's clean air regime with the 1990 Clean Air Act.

Therefore, in light of the environmental social movement of the 1960s and early 1970s and the growth of environmental awareness among the American public, corporate America has not taken a confrontational tact toward the existence of environmental regulations, per se. Instead, it has been content with attempting to determine the content of these regulations, and in many important regards the corporate community has been highly successful in this endeavor. Hence, while Cahn (1995) provides little insight into the nature of the policymaking process, his assessment of the largely symbolic content of post-1970 environmental regulatory policies can be viewed as correct. Cahn's conclusion is based on his analysis of the federal government's policies on air pollution abatement, water quality, waste management, and energy consumption. The symbolic nature of environmental regulatory policies is also reflected in their lax enforcement (Mintz 1995; Cushman 1998; Weber 1998, chap. 3). Therefore, whether by design or happenstance, the public is given the symbolism of environmental legislation while the business community is provided with tangible public policies (Edelman 1964). In this way, the environmental social movement and the public's environmental concerns are managed, and the relationship between corporate firms and the environment is only minimally altered.

NOTES

1. For a discussion of the health effects of air pollutants, see Bryner (1995, chap. 2).

2. Despite this reduction of automotive emissions, automobile emissions continue to pose serious health and environmental risks because there are more automobiles on the road and people are driving longer distances than in the 1960s (U.S. Congress 1990b, 227 and 231).

3. In 1989, the automotive and oil industries initiated a joint research project designed to find cleaner-burning fuels for cars and trucks. The Big Three automobile companies participated in the project, as did the nation's fourteen largest oil refiners (Brown, 18 October 1989).

4. I would like to thank G. William Domhoff for making these, and other, internal CAWG documents available to me.

5. Bryner (1997) opines that "even more difficult than making the economic calculations [necessary to implement a pollution tax program] may be mobilizing sufficient political power to overcome industry opposition to pollution charges" (91).

6. Ellerman and his associates (2000, 172–73) report that while a market for emission permits has been established, the level of trading is substantially below expectations. This means it is debatable, if not doubtful, whether the reduction in sulfur dioxide emissions from power plants since the passage of the 1990 Clean Air Act can be attributed to the permit trading system. Instead, Ellerman et al. (2000) argue that the proximate cause for much of the reduction in sulfur dioxide emissions from midwestern and Appalachian power plants is the drop in rail transportation costs that resulted from railroad deregulation. This lowering of transportation costs made low-sulfur coal mined mostly in the West more price competitive in relation to the high-sulfur coal extracted in the Midwest and Appalachia.

7. Under the 1977 amendments to the Clean Air Act, the provisions that applied to coal-burning power plants only applied to power plants that were to be built in the future.

8. Overall, the House version of the 1990 Clean Air Act fared much better in the Senate–House conference committee than did the Senate version (Cohen 1995, 174–75).

9. In addition to opposition from the oil industry (U.S. Congress 1990b, 368), the automobile industry also opposed this provision of the Bush administration bill because it mandated that they build "clean fuel" cars without the certainty that there was a market for these automobiles (U.S. Congress 1990b, 366).

10. According to Charles Gray, EPA director of emissions control technology, "They [the oil industry] originally put out reformulated gas to sidetrack the idea of alternative fuels" (as quoted in Babcock and Weisskopf, 22 May 1990). Furthermore, Wald (25 September 199) reports that with respect to the reformulated gasoline provision in the House bill, "At the urging of the oil industry, [House] staff members said, the House had drafted a law that would allow oil companies to use either the House's recipe for gasoline or any equally clean gasoline" (A24).

11. Other cities can opt into the program.

12. The EPA's ability to monitor compliance with the reformulated gasoline standards is hampered by the fact that the oil industry was successful in having the federal government use an averaging scheme to measure compliance, as opposed to a gallon-by-gallon approach (Weber 1998, chap. 5; Gonzalez 1999).

13. The California pilot program was never implemented.

14. The Senate version of the 1990 Clean Air Act did mandate the use of ethanol as a fuel additive. This provision, however, was supplanted in the Conference Committee by the House version. The House provision did not mandate any fuel additives (Adler 1992).

15. In addition to those provisions of the 1990 Clean Air Act already discussed, this legislation set standards for 189 hazardous chemicals (Title III). The act, however, allows extensions and exemptions that provide the EPA administrator significant discretion. It requires, for example, that the best available technology be used to reduce the emissions of the toxic chemicals listed in legislation. When applying these rules, however, the EPA must take into consideration the cost associated with these regulations as well as the expected health benefits. The 1990 Clean Air Act also allows the EPA to add or delete from the list of toxic emissions to be regulated.

Additionally, the act mandates specific pollution controls for stationary sources to be applied in ozone nonattainment areas and establishes new mandatory attainment deadlines for urban and regional areas (Title I). Without the necessary rules on automobile and industrial emissions, however, it is questionable whether the attainment deadlines established for urban regional areas can be achieved.

Furthermore, the federal government's newest automobile emission standards, including those on light trucks, were also prompted by policy changes on the state level—especially in California, New York, and Massachusetts (Perez-Pena, 7 November 1999).

16. For a critique of market-based regulatory approaches, see Dowie (1995, 109–18).

Conclusion
Political Power and the Environment

In this study I have argued that corporate decision makers and other persons of wealth (i.e., economic elites) have been the most powerful influence in the management of the national forests and the national parks, as well as in the development of federal wilderness preservation and federal clean air policies. Therefore, in all four areas I hold that the plural elite/economic elite perspective provides the deepest insight into state behavior and public policy development.

Hence, despite the professionalism and expanded state structures of the U.S. Forest Service and the National Park Service, these agencies did not behave autonomously as suggested by state autonomy theory. Furthermore, looking through the prism of political economy, we can see how both the federal government's forestry and national park polices benefited the economic elite in general. In the case of federal forest policies, economic elites and corporate interests successfully used the federal government's resources to help mold the profession of forestry into conceptualizing forests as "crops" rather than "wilderness." In the case of federal national park policies, corporate interests were served by bringing "economically useless" wilderness into the marketplace of useful properties through public ownership and management. Thus, the forest and park service case studies document that economic and corporate elites have actively and successfully promoted certain federal environmental policies to create new long-term opportunities for profit making.

Klyza (1992), for one, argues that the forest service was an autonomous agency during the Progressive era. A factor that prompts him to find state autonomy in the case of the early forest service was the professionalism of this agency. Specifically, according to Klyza, it was pursuing the public good as defined by professional forestry. He contends:

> The drive for autonomy by the forestry agency during this period [1898–1910] was based on a coherent conception of the public interest. The idea was that the public interest was best served by having the government retain ownership of large tracts of forest, and that forests be managed for the greatest good of all of

society by foresters (technical experts) in the employ of the federal government. This idea of technocratic utilitarianism can be traced back to Germany, a center of forestry in Europe. (179)

To arrive at the conclusion that the early forest service, and its precursors, were pursuing the public interest, Klyza uncritically accepts these agencies' definition of this interest. This allows him to avoid the class origins and biases of practical forestry and how it informs the forest service's professionalism. Furthermore, Klyza fails to analyze the forest service's policies with regard to the management of the national forests. Such an analysis would lead to the conclusion that the management of the national forests for "the greatest good of all of society" has meant throughout the history of the forest service managing these forests to the benefit of the timber industry (Robbins 1982; Hirt 1994).

In our wilderness preservation case studies, it was members of the economic elite who provided the necessary political resources to have the wilderness areas in question (i.e., Yosemite Park, Jackson Hole, and Redwood National Park) incorporated into the national park system. It was also found that connections to members of the economic elite have historically had a significant impact on the policy goals and the political discourses of environmental groups. Both of these factors strongly indicate that a significant portion of the wilderness preservation network has historically operated like an economic elite–led policy-planning network.

Moreover, the Redwood National Park case study demonstrates how corporate and economic elites successfully blocked an environmental initiative that was advanced by a strong state agency (i.e., the National Park Service) and that received organized public support. Corporate interests were able to deflect and redefine this initiative in such a way that it no longer contravened their long-term interest in maintaining control over investment (i.e., supremacy of private property rights) and forced a reconfiguration of the proposal to insure that its short-term interests (timber profits) were not threatened by the proposed park. The result was a less than viable park that failed to achieve the main goals of state officials or environmental groups. Moreover, the large timber firms that contributed lands to the Redwood National Park were amply compensated for these largely cut-over lands.

As explained in chapter 1, Nash (1982) finds pluralism in the formation of national park and wilderness preservation policies. Specifically, he holds that both national park and wilderness preservation policies have in many regards been strongly influenced by wilderness activists. These activists, according to Nash, have, especially in more recent times, been able to tap into a growing desire among the U.S. public for natural landscapes to achieve their policy goals.

Nash, however, finds pluralism in the policy areas of national park management and wilderness preservation by downplaying or ignoring central historical and theoretically relevant factors. First, he downplays or ignores the extent to which economic interests (e.g., railroads, automobile manufacturers, and local developers) have led in the creation of national parks from lands that would otherwise be economically useless. These interests have historically sought to develop these lands, which had few economically viable natural resources, into profit-generating tourist attractions (Runte 1997). Second, Nash ignores the extent to which many supporters of pristine wilderness have been dissatisfied with the park service's management of the national parks. This dissatisfaction stems largely from the service's development of the parks and its emphasis on the promotion of tourism. Third, Nash ignores the key leadership that economic elites provided in the preservation of the federal government's most controversial wilderness (i.e., Jackson Hole and Redwood National Park).

In my final case, federal clean air policies demonstrate that even during periods of large-scale public mobilization that enjoy political support within the state, corporate and economic elites can successfully dilute and delay apparently progressive environmental policies to the extent that their consequences are mainly symbolic, while shifting much of the actual costs of implementation from polluters to consumers (e.g., catalytic converters). Additionally, the most substantial expansion of federal clean air regulations (i.e., the 1990 Clean Air Act) was promoted and shaped by corporate elites seeking to stabilize the political and regulatory milieu in which the economy operates.

Both Bryner (1995) and Kraft (1994) offer different interpretations of the policy formulation process that created the 1990 Clean Air Act. As noted in chapter 1, Bryner's is consistent with pluralism, and Kraft's with the issue network/state autonomy view. Neither of them, however, take into account the state and local regulations that prompted the corporate community to support new federal clean air legislation. It is only by ignoring this factor that Kraft can argue that officials, such as Representative John Dingell, were behaving autonomously of the automobile industry when they helped formulate and support the 1990 Clean Air Act. As discussed in chapter 6, Dingell was and is a longtime ally of this industry.

Furthermore, Bryner, in particular, mistakenly argues that the corporate community was fragmented on the issue of clean air policy. Specifically, he writes:

> Given industries' economic clout, ranging from honoraria paid to members to campaign contributions, one might expect that lobbyists could have freely worked their will in the legislative process. But business lobbying is rarely, if ever, united, since competitive pressures cut in many different directions. (135)

Bryner, however, largely ignores the Clean Air Working Group, and its successful effort to coordinate business lobbying and political activity on the issue of clean air. Despite the fact that the CAWG was industry's key coordinating and lobbying group, Bryner only makes cursory reference to it (103–4) in his extensive analysis of the 1990 Clean Air Act legislative process (1995, chap. 3).

AN ANALYSIS OF COMPETING POLICYMAKING MODELS

Issue Networks

Why have the other policymaking models used throughout this analysis failed to offer adequate frameworks to analyze these policy areas? The issue network perspective, for instance, suffers from the same flaws as does early pluralism. Noneconomic elite actors do not have the political resources necessary to compete effectively in the public policy formation process. The significant difference between early pluralism and the concept of issue networks is that the latter approach reduces the expected impact of citizen groups on the policymaking process. Pluralism argues that noneconomic elite groups can extract significant policy concessions from the corporate community and the state through the policymaking process. The issue network perspective contends that issue network members, by expanding the scope of conflict, only change the "nature" of public policy outcomes. If, however, the issue networks surrounding our four policy areas did modify policy outputs, the groups and individuals representing the noneconomic elite perspectives were dissatisfied with these changes. To expand meaningfully the scope of conflict prospective antagonists must have the power to "force" policy changes.

A major reason that noneconomic actors do not have the required resources to expand the scope of conflict, or extract policy concessions, is because votes throughout American history have only had a sporadic effect on the policymaking process. Votes are the most important resource that political actors could potentially and reliably utilize against the economic elite within the policy formulation process. The primary reason that votes have only infrequently served as a counterweight to the political resources of wealth and income is the weakness of American political parties.

Given the fact that American political parties are nonideological and unable to discipline candidates once they are in office, parties are largely ineffective channels through which voters can register their public policy preferences into the policymaking process. Furthermore, the nebulous nature of U.S. political parties, and subsequently elections, means that the American electoral system does a poor job of educating and mobilizing the public on political and social issues. Additionally, the fact that parties cannot discipline candidates once they are in office means that with regard to those few public policy promises made by candidates there is no system in place to ensure that they will follow through. This leads to further mistrust and alienation on the part of voters and makes it more difficult for public interest groups to mobilize voters on behalf of their public policy issues (Burnham 1982; Polsby 1983; Ware 1996; Wattenberg 1991; Monroe 2001).

The issue network/state autonomy perspective suffers from another flaw. Specifically, it argues that science can dictate policy outcomes. Therefore, the issue network/state autonomy theorists contend that autonomous scientific experts play a central role in the policymaking process. Science, however, is malleable (Noble 1977). This is what I found in the case of forestry. While members of the economic elite realized the need to manage the exploitation of forests, the timber industry rejected the two forest management paradigms offered at the time: forest preservation and European forestry. As a result, members of the economic elite erected a policy network and reconfigured European forestry into practical forestry—an approach that conformed to the policy goals of the timber industry.

Our other case studies demonstrate that science and experts cannot compete with the power of the economic elite. It is that view of the national parks that emphasizes their economic use that is prioritized within federal park policy and not that view that values the parks for their pristine wilderness. The former policy is promoted by the corporate groups that economically benefit from tourism to the parks, and the latter by wilderness advocates and academicians. Furthermore, the preferences of the large timber firms in northern California determined the contours of Redwood National Park, not those of the environmental groups that led the fight to preserve the redwood. The environmental groups were guided in their preferences by two distinct scientific approaches to wilderness preservation. Finally, those policy proposals put forth by environmental lobbyists and EPA scientists that did not correspond to the policy preferences of the corporate community were not included in the 1990 Clean Air Act.

The instrumental nature of science and experts points to a key point of contention between Domhoff's policy-planning network concept, Heclo's issue networks, and Skocpol's polity-centered approach. What Heclo and Skocpol identify as autonomous issue networks, or part of an autonomous polity, Domhoff contends is part of an economic elite–dominated policy-planning network. While Skocpol argues that issue networks are the conduits through which autonomous scientific discourses are developed and incorporated into the policymaking process, Domhoff views these networks as arenas through which scientific discourses are reconciled with the class interests of the economic elite. This study has found that members of the economic elite have the ability to recast scientific discourses, and to pick and chose among experts and policy ideas. In turn, these reconfigured discourses, and favored experts and ideas, are incorporated into public policy.

State Autonomy Theory

Turning the discussion specifically to state autonomy theory, this study exposes two substantial flaws in this analytical approach. One, the theoretical concept of the state employed by state theorists is empirically untenable. Two, the claim made by these theorists that bureaucratic capacity is an indicator of autonomy or potential autonomy is also empirically faulty.

Timothy Mitchell (1991), in his excellent critique of the state autonomy approach, concludes that while the state is conceptualized by state autonomy theorists as a coherent discrete entity, they fail to make their case empirically. He specifically points out that "the statist approach always begins from the assumption that the state is a distinct entity, opposed to and set apart from a larger entity called society" (89). As demonstrated throughout this book, however, "the edges of the state are uncertain; societal elements seem to penetrate it on all sides, and the resulting boundary between state and society is difficult to determine" (Mitchell 1991, 88).

The myth of the state as standing apart from society serves to mask the biases of state actors and policies. As a result, the class backgrounds and class ties of such policymakers as Chief Forester Gifford Pinchot, park service directors Stephen Mather and Horace Albright, presidential adviser Laurence Rockefeller, and John Dingell are often ignored or minimized. Mitchell (1991) argues that "the appearance that state and society are separate things is part of the way a given financial and economic order is maintained" (90).

The myth of the "discrete state" goes as follows: The state, as a distinct public institution, serves the public interest. By implication state actors, by adopting official rubrics, adopt a society-wide perspective that prompts them to pursue the "public good." The public grousing of economic elites, and their spokespersons, over the state helps to perpetuate the mythic separation of state and society. The discrete state myth works to reify the state and the actors within it.

Indicative of this reification, manifestations of wealth in the policymaking process, such as campaign finance, gifts, or the promise of lucrative employment after government service, are often viewed as obstacles to a state that would otherwise serve the public interest. Instead, however, these manifestations are more likely part of the cultivation of a state that responds to the policy preferences of economic elites at the expense of workers, consumers, small businesses, and public interest advocates. We saw that John D. Rockefeller, Jr. gave cash gifts to Horace Albright, when the latter was a policymaker in the park service. These gifts, in turn, contributed to the loyalty and responsiveness that Albright developed toward Rockefeller. In the case of the 1990 Clean Air Act, the years of campaign finance provided by industry groups resulted in a House and Senate that prioritized these groups' policy preferences. In contrast, the policy preferences and proposals of environmental lobbyists and EPA officials were given peripheral importance.

State autonomy theorists explicitly incorporate the discrete state myth into their analytical framework (Mitchell 1991, 91). When Klyza (1992), for example, provides his analysis of the early U.S. Forest Service, he ignores Pinchot's class and social background and his participation in the practical forestry policy network. The theoretical implication of this omission is that Pinchot's class and social background, and professional relationships, did not affect his decisions as chief forester. The state autonomy approach assumes that if state officials are not obstructed by outside groups and possess the requisite expertise and organizational resources, they will pursue the public good or, put another way, the national interest.[1]

It is in this context that the notion of a weak versus strong state becomes an issue (Skocpol 1985; Barrow 1993, 130–36). Strong states are those that are bureaucratically developed, centralized, and professionalized. Weak states, or weak state structures, are those that are underfunded and fragmented, and appointments to them are determined by patronage. Thus, it is argued by state autonomy theorists that state officials, empowered via strong state structures, can pursue the public good as defined by scientific discourses. Klyza (1996) makes this precise argument in his book on federal land management. He contends that because the policy regimes of mining and grazing on the federal lands are implemented by weak state structures, these regimes serve the interests of producer groups at the expense of the public good. In contrast, Klyza argues that the management of the federal forests is conducted by the strong state structure of the forest service. Therefore, he reasons that forest service policies pursue the public interest as determined by professional forestry, or the scientific discourse of "technocratic utilitarianism" (i.e., practical forestry) (1992; 1996, 74–76).

In describing the autonomy of the service during the Progressive era, Klyza (1992) emphasizes its increased resources and bureaucratic capacities:

> Following the transfer [of the forest reserves], the Forest Service was reorganized so that it would have this management capacity. The most important major themes of this newly organized Forest Service were the emphasis on both efficient and scientific management, decentralization, and the fostering of a spirit of commitment to public service among the employees of the Forest Service. The agency was quite successful in achieving these goals.
>
> The increased capability of the Forest Service is also reflected in the remarkable growth from 1899 through 1908 in the agency's budget and in the number of its employees [as discussed in chap. 2]. Despite *these successes in achieving and increasing autonomy*, this window of opportunity would not remain open long [emphasis added]. (185–86)

Therefore, reflective of the strong state concept rooted within state autonomy theory, Klyza argues that the increasing management capacity and resources of the forest service provided it the ability to behave autonomously.

As I described in chapter 2, however, the forest service's bureaucratic expansion and development did not lead to its autonomy. Instead, the forest service received an increasing amount of resources and expanded bureaucratically only because it initiated policies that served the interests of the timber industry. Additionally, the National Park Service grew and flourished because of programs that served economic interests. The park service's budget grew, for example, with expanded road building programs in the 1930s, and again in the 1950s and 1960s with the long-term development program entitled Mission 66. Hence, the cases of the forest and park services demonstrate that bureaucratic development and increasing institutional resources are not necessarily indicators of political autonomy but, quite the contrary, can be indicators of nonautonomy and political subservience to specific interests.

THE IMPLICATIONS OF ECONOMIC ELITE DOMINANCE FOR THE ENVIRONMENT

Vos (1997) argues that the environmental politics literature has three dominant approaches to analyzing the relationship between the natural environment and humanity (also see Dryzek 1997). These approaches are the free market approach, ecological science advocacy, and deep ecology. (Here I will treat the first two.) The core difference between these paradigms is rooted in the following issue: What are the most appropriate means to manage the natural environment and achieve a sustainable environment?

The free market approach to sustainability argues that a sustainable society can be achieved by relying on the price signals provided by the market. These price signals indicate that a particular resource is becoming relatively scarce, and in response to these price signals, societal actors will respond with appropriate husbandry measures. Additionally, increasing prices associated with resource depletion will provide incentives to develop technologies that either create substitutes for the depleted resource or induce a more efficient and sustainable utilization of the resource in question. Therefore, the key to achieving sustainability for free market advocates is to establish property rights and, subsequently, markets for natural resources. Through this creation and maintenance of markets, we can harness the energy and ingenuity derived from the pursuit of self-interest and channel them into the development of a sustainable society.

While the free market advocates tout the infinite possibilities when humankind's intellect and initiative are tapped by market forces, ecological science advocates, according to Vos, focus on the finite nature of the natural environment. Ecological science advocates argue that regardless of the limitless potential of humanity, natural resources are finite and that this human potential will invariably run up against the limitations of the environment. In light of this limit, ecological science advocates believe that there needs to be some type of intervention to ensure that economic and population growth do not overrun the capabilities of the earth to support life (e.g., Milbrath 1989). Additionally, ecological science proponents seriously question the ability of technology to overcome the constraints placed on humanity by nature. As such, they strongly caution against placing all of our faith in the creation of new technologies to rescue humankind from potential environmental disasters created by excessive exploitation and disregard for the limited capacities of environmental sinks to regenerate natural resources. Also, ecological science advocates point to the difficulty of establishing property rights over several important resources, as well as the negative environmental effects of privatizing certain resources.

In light of these competing paradigms, the political dominance of the economic elite has two implications. First, the continued dominance of this group means that the relationship between humankind and the environment will be primarily mediated by the market. The economic elite as discussed throughout this book is akin to the Marxist notion of the capitalist class. Via its ownership of the means of production, the economic elite derives its dominant economic, political, and social position from the exploitation of labor and natural resources. This exploitation takes place largely through the operation of the market. Thus, as long as the economic elite remain the dominant political force in society, and the market continues to serve this group's class interests, the free market approach will be the paradigm that predominantly describes humanity's relationship to the natural environment (Carter 1999).

What does this mean for public health and the health of the environment? It means that these concerns will be relegated to secondary status below the operation of the market and the class interests of the economic elite. Furthermore, most attempts by environmental groups to replace the logic of the market with social or environmental values will have only limited success. In this regard, we have to hope that the free market advocates are correct and that the market can provide for a sustainable environment.

The second implication of economic elite political dominance is that ecological science advocates have only had a limited and sporadic effect on environmental policy in the United States. Instead, in most instances where the federal government has intervened to manage a natural resource, this intervention has been largely guided by economic elites and producer groups who were seeking to gain an economic advantage by circumventing the market. We saw this with the management of the national forests and the national parks. Foss (1960) also observes this with the federal government's management of livestock grazing on the public domain. Furthermore, as discussed by Cahn (1995), the federal government's most important environmental regulatory policies can be viewed as more symbolic than substantive.

Therefore, in conclusion, the political dominance of the nation's economic elite has both normative and practical implications. This dominance violates broadly held democratic notions of equal representation and participation (Dryzek 1996). Moreover, the political dominance of the economic elite, coupled with its class interests, places substantial constraints on society's ability to confront and deal with potentially devastating environmental problems.

NOTE

1. An important addendum here is that state autonomy adherents view the incorporation of scientific discourses into the policymaking process as more theoretically relevant than examining the political implications of policy outputs. After examining the work of various state autonomy theorists, Mitchell (1991) concludes that the concept of the national, or public, interest as posited by these theorists "must be construed not in relation to any broader commercial or political interests, but as the state's independent desire" (87). Therefore, what becomes paramount for state theorists is not how a particular notion of the public interest, or a particular scientific discourse, affects different groups and individuals but whether such notions are willingly embraced by officials within the state.

Bibliography

Ackerman, Bruce, and William T. Hassler. 1981. *Clean Coal/Dirty Air*. New Haven, Conn.: Yale University Press.

Adler, Jonathan H. 1992. "Clean Fuels, Dirty Air." In *Environmental Politics: Public Costs, Private Rewards*, ed. Michael S. Grave and Fred L. Smith, Jr. New York: Praeger.

Albright, Horace M. 2 September 1924. "To John D. Rockefeller, Jr." Sleepy Hollow, N.Y.: Rockefeller Archive Center.

———. 4 January 1927. "To John D. Rockefeller, Jr." Sleepy Hollow, N.Y.: Rockefeller Archive Center.

———. 15 January 1929. "To John D. Rockefeller, Jr." Sleepy Hollow, N.Y.: Rockefeller Archive Center.

———. 11 March 1930. "To John D. Rockefeller, Jr." Sleepy Hollow, N.Y.: Rockefeller Archive Center.

———. 22 July 1939. "To John D. Rockefeller, Jr." Sleepy Hollow, N.Y.: Rockefeller Archive Center.

———. 26 March 1941. "To Mrs. John D. Rockefeller, Jr." Sleepy Hollow, N.Y.: Rockefeller Archive Center.

———. 23 January 1947. "To John D. Rockefeller, Jr." Sleepy Hollow, N.Y.: Rockefeller Archive Center.

———. 9 December 1953. "To John D. Rockefeller, Jr." Sleepy Hollow, N.Y.: Rockefeller Archive Center.

———. 25 January 1954. "To John D. Rockefeller, Jr." Sleepy Hollow, N.Y.: Rockefeller Archive Center.

Albright, Horace, and Robert Cahn. 1985. *The Birth of the National Park Service: The Founding Years, 1913–33*. Chicago: Howe.

Albright, Horace, and Marian Albright Schenck. 1999. *Creating the National Park Service: The Missing Years*. Norman: University of Oklahoma Press.

Allin, Craig. 1982. *The Politics of Wilderness Preservation*. Westport, Conn.: Greenwood.

Almond, Gabriel A. 1988. "The Return to the State." *American Political Science Review* 82 (September): 853–74.

American Forestry Association. 1905. *Proceedings of the American Forest Congress: Held at Washington, D.C., January 2 to 6, 1905, under the Auspices of the American Forestry Association*. Washington, D.C.: Suter.

Andrews, Richard N. L. 1999. *Managing the Environment, Managing Ourselves: A History of American Environmental Policy*. New Haven, Conn.: Yale University Press.

Babcock, Charles R., and Michael Weisskopf. 22 May 1990. " 'Clean Gasoline' Pact Unveiled." *Washington Post*, p. A1.

Baden, John, and Tim O'Brien. 1997. "Bringing Private Management to the Public Lands: Environmental and Economic Advantages." In *Flash Points in Environmental Policymaking: Controversies in Achieving Sustainability*, ed. Sheldon Kamieniecki, George A. Gonzalez, and Robert O. Vos. Albany: State University of New York Press.

Barringer, Mark. 1999. "Mission Impossible: National Park Development in the 1950s." *Journal of the West* 38 (January): 22–26.

Barrow, Clyde W. 1990. *Universities and the Capitalist State: Corporate Liberalism and the Reconstruction of American Higher Education, 1894–1928*. Madison: University of Wisconsin Press.

———. 1992. "Corporate Liberalism, Finance Hegemony, and Central State Intervention in the Reconstruction of American Higher Education." *Studies in American Political Development* 6 (Fall): 420–44.

———. 1993. *Critical Theories of the State*. Madison: University of Wisconsin Press.

———. 2001. "The Miliband–Poulantzas Debate: An Intellectual History." In *Rethinking the State: Miliband, Poulantzas, and State Theory*, ed. Stanley Aronowitz and Peter Bratsis. Minneapolis: University of Minnesota Press.

Bates, J. Leonard. 1957. "Fulfilling American Democracy: The Conservation Movement, 1907 to 1921." *Mississippi Valley Historical Review* 44 (June): 29–57.

Baumgartner, Frank, and Bryan Jones. 1993. *Agendas and Instability in American Politics*. Chicago: University of Chicago Press.

Baumgartner, Frank, and Beth L. Leech. 1998. *Basic Interests: The Importance of Groups in Politics and in Political Science*. Princeton, N.J.: Princeton University Press.

Bauer, Raymond A., Ithiel de Sola Pool, and Lewis Anthony Dexter. 1972. *American Business and Public Policy*. Chicago: Aldine Atherton.

Berry, Jeffrey. 1977. *Lobbying for the People*. Princeton, N.J.: Princeton University Press.

Block, Fred. 1990. *Postindustrial Possibilities: A Critique of Economic Discourse*. Los Angeles: University of California Press.

Bosso, Christopher. 1987. *Pesticides and Politics: The Life Cycle of a Public Issue*. Pittsburgh, Pa.: University of Pittsburgh Press.

Braadbaart, Okke. 1998. "American Bias in Environmental Economics: Industrial Pollution Abatement and 'Incentives versus Regulations.' " *Environmental Politics* 7 (Summer): 134–52.

Bradsher, Keith. 13 July 1999. "2.2 Million Toyotas Violate Clean Air Act, U.S. Suit Says." *New York Times*, p. A1.

Brandis, Dietrich. 9 August 1897. "To Gifford Pinchot," in the Gifford Pinchot Papers. Washington, D.C.: Library of Congress.

Brown, Warren. 18 October 1989. "Auto, Oil Industries to Search for Cleaner-Burning Fuels." *Washington Post*, p. F3.

Browne, William P. 1995. *Cultivating Congress: Constituents, Issues, and Interests in Agriculture Policymakers*. Lawrence: University of Kansas Press.

Bryner, Gary C. 1995. *Blue Skies, Green Politics: The Clean Air Act of 1990 and Its Implementation*. Washington, D.C.: Congressional Quarterly Press.

———. 1997. "Market Incentives in Air Pollution Control." In *Flash Points in Environmental Policymaking: Controversies in Achieving Sustainability*, ed. Sheldon Kamieniecki, George A. Gonzalez, and Robert O. Vos. Albany, N.Y.: State University of New York Press.

Burch Jr., Philip H. 1980/81. *Elites in American History*, vols. 1–3. New York: Holmes & Meier.

Burnham, Walter Dean. 1982. *The Current Crisis in American Politics*. New York: Oxford University Press.

Burtraw, Dallas. 1996. "Trading Emissions to Clean the Air: Exchanges Few but Savings Many." *Resources for the Future* 122 (Winter): 3–6.

Cahn, Matthew A. 1995. *Environmental Deceptions: The Tension between Liberalism and Environmental Policymaking in the United States*. Albany: State University of New York Press.

"California Adopts New Car Emission Rules." 30 September 1990. *New York Times*, sect. 1, p. 24.

Carter, Alan. 1999. *A Radical Green Political Theory*. New York: Routledge.

Christoff, Peter. 1996. "Ecological Modernization, Ecological Modernities." *Environmental Politics* 5: 476–500.

Clarke, Jeanne N., and Daniel McCool. 1996. *Staking Out the Terrain*. 2d ed. Albany: State University of New York Press.

Clean Air Working Group. 1981a. "The Clean Air Working Group." In the Douglas Soutar Papers. Ithaca, N.Y.: Cornell University: M. P. Catherwood Library, Collection 5914, Box 8.

———. 1981b. "Summary of Position on Priority Recommendations for Amendments to the Clean Air Act." In the Douglas Soutar Papers. Ithaca, N.Y.: Cornell University: M. P. Catherwood Library, Collection 5914, Box 8.

Cohen, Michael P. 1988. *The History of the Sierra Club, 1892–1970*. San Francisco: Sierra Club Books.

Cohen, Richard E. 27 October 1990. "Settling Something: The Clean Air Bill." *National Journal*, p. 2616.

———. 1995. *Washington at Work: Back Rooms and Clean Air*. Boston: Allyn & Bacon.

Collier, Peter, and David Horowitz. 1976. *The Rockefellers: An American Dynasty*. New York: Holt, Rinehart, & Winston.

"Colorado's High-Oxygen Fuel Test Runs Smoothly." 1 March 1988. *New York Times*, p. B5.

Cushman, John H., Jr. 7 June 1998. "E.P.A. and States Found to Be Lax on Pollution Law." *New York Times*, p. 1.

Dahl, Robert A., and Charles E. Lindblom. 1953. *Politics, Economics, and Welfare*. New Haven, Conn.: Yale University Press.

Dahl, Robert A., 1956. *A Preface to Democratic Theory*. Chicago: University of Chicago Press.

———. 1989. *Democracy and Its Critics*. New Haven, Conn.: Yale University Press.

———. 1961. *Who Governs?: Democracy and Power in an American City*. New Haven, Conn.: Yale University Press.

Dahl, Robert A., and Charles E. Lindblom. 1976. "Preface." In *Politics, Economics, and Welfare*. New Haven, Conn.: Yale University Press.

Dana, Samuel T., and Sally K. Fairfax. 1980. *Forest and Range Policy*. New York: McGraw-Hill.

Davis, Charles. 1997. "Politics and Public Rangeland Policy." In *Western Public Lands and Environmental Politics*, ed. Charles Davis. Boulder, Colo.: Westview.

Dilsaver, Lary, and William C. Tweed. 1990. *Challenge of the Big Trees of Kings Canyon and Sequoia National Parks*. Three Rivers, Calif.: Sequoia National History Association.

Domhoff, G. William. 1974. *The Bohemian Grove and Other Retreats: A Study in Ruling-Class Cohesiveness*. New York: Harper & Row.

———. 1978. *The Powers That Be*. New York: Random House.

———. 1987. "Where Do Government Experts Come From?" In *Power Elites and Organizations*, ed. G. William Domhoff and Thomas R. Dye. Beverly Hills, Calif.: Sage.

———. 1990. *The Power Elite and the State*. New York: Aldine de Gruyter.

———. 1996. *State Autonomy or Class Dominance? Case Studies on Policy Making in America*. New York: Aldine de Gruyter.

———. 1998. *Who Rules America? Power and Politics in the Year 2000*. 3d ed. Mountain View, Calif.: Mayfield.

Dowie, Mark. 1995. *Losing Ground: American Environmentalism at the Close of the Twentieth Century*. Cambridge, Mass.: MIT Press.

Dryzek, John. 1996. *Democracy in Capitalist Times*. New York: Oxford University Press.

———. 1997. *The Politics of the Earth: Environmental Discourses*. New York: Oxford University Press.

Dye, Thomas R. 1990. *Who's Running America? The Bush Era*. Englewood Cliffs, N.J.: Prentice Hall.

Eakins, David. 1969. "Business Planners and America's Postwar Expansion." In *Corporations and the Cold War*, ed. David Horowitz. New York: Monthly Review Press.

———. 1972. "Policy-Planning for the Establishment." In *A New History of Leviathan*, ed. Ronald Radosh and Murray N. Rothbard. New York: Dutton.

Edelman, Murray. 1964. *The Symbolic Uses of Politics*. Urbana: University of Illinois Press.

———. 1971. *Politics as Symbolic Action: Mass Arousal and Quiescence*. Chicago: Markham.

———. 1988. *Constructing the Political Spectacle*. Chicago: University of Chicago Press.

Ellerman, A. Denny, Paul L. Joskow, Richard Schmalensee, Juan-Pablo Montero, and Elizabeth M. Bailey. 2000. *Markets for Clean Air: The U.S. Acid Rain Program*. Cambridge: Cambridge University Press.

Ernst, Joseph W. 1991a. "Epilogue." *Worthwhile Places*, ed. Joseph W. Ernst. New York: Fordham University Press, 337–341.

———. 1991b. "An Overview." *Worthwhile Places*, ed. Joseph W. Ernst. New York: Fordham University Press, 3–20.

———. 1991c. "Preface." *Worthwhile Places*, ed. Joseph W. Ernst. New York: Fordham University Press, 1–2.

———, ed. 1991d. *Worthwhile Places*. New York: Fordham University Press.

Everhart, William C. 1983. *The National Park Service*. Boulder, Colo.: Westview.

Feagin, Joe R., Anthony M. Orum, and Gideon Sjoberg. 1991. *A Case for the Case Study*. Chapel Hill: University of North Carolina Press.

Finegold, Kenneth, and Theda Skocpol. 1995. *State and Party in America's New Deal*. Madison: University of Wisconsin Press.

Foresta, Ronald A. 1984. *America's National Parks and Their Keepers*. Washington, D.C.: Resources for the Future.

Foss, Phillip O. 1960. *Politics and Grass.* Seattle: University of Washington.

Frome, Michael. 1974. *Battle for the Wilderness.* New York: Praeger.

———. 1992. *Regreening the National Parks.* Tucson: University of Arizona Press.

Frothingham, E. H. 1941 May. "Biltmore—Fountain-Head of Forestry in America." *American Forests* 47: 215–17.

Gold, Allan R. 30 October 1990. "Critics say Cars got Break on Clean Air." *New York Times,* p. A18.

Gonzalez, George A. 1998. "The Conservation Policy Network, 1890–1910: The Development and Implementation of 'Practical' Forestry." *Polity* 31 (Winter): 269–99.

———. 1999. "Book Review of *Pluralism by the Rules,* by Edward P. Weber." *American Political Science Review* 93 (June): 461–62.

Gorz, Andre. 1994. *Capitalism, Socialism, Ecology.* New York: Norton.

Gottlieb, Robert, Maureen Smith, Julie Roque, and Pamela Yates. 1995. "New Approaches to Toxics: Production Design, Right-to-Know, and Definition Debates." In *Reducing Toxics: A New Approach to Policy and Industrial Decisionmaking,* ed. Robert Gottlieb. Washington, D.C.: Island.

Gould, Lewis. 1988. *Lady Bird Johnson and the Environment.* Lawrence: University of Kansas Press.

———. 1999. *Lady Bird Johnson: Our Environmental First Lady.* Lawrence: University of Kansas Press.

Graf, William L. 1990. *Wilderness Preservation and the Sagebrush Rebellions.* Savage, Md.: Rowman & Littlefield.

Graves, Henry S. 1901. "The Study and Practice of Silviculture." *The Forester* 7 (May): 102–15.

Hager, George. 23 September 1989. "Bush Scores Early Victory in Clean Air Markup." *Congressional Quarterly Weekly Report,* pp. 2451–52.

———. 30 September 1989. "Waxman, Dingell Talk Truce on Auto Emissions Rules." *Congressional Quarterly Weekly Report,* pp. 2551–52.

———. 7 October 1989. "Energy Panel Seals Pact on Vehicle Pollution." *Congressional Quarterly Weekly Report,* pp. 2621–24.

———. 14 October 1989. "Bush's Plan for Cleaner Fuels Scaled Back by House Panel." *Congressional Quarterly Weekly Report,* pp. 2700–01.

———. 21 October 1989. "Tougher Air-Toxics Standards Get Quick Nod from Panel." *Congressional Quarterly Weekly Report,* pp. 2783–84.

———. 28 October 1989. "Senate Panel One-Ups Bush on Clean Air Controls." *Congressional Quarterly Weekly Report,* pp. 2864–68.

———. 18 November 1990. "Senate Stage is Finally Set for Clean-Air Showdown." *Congressional Quarterly Weekly Report,* pp. 3145–47.

———. 20 January 1990. "For Industry and Opponents, a Showdown Is in the Air." *Congressional Quarterly Weekly Report,* pp. 145–47.

———. 10 February 1990. "Closed-Door Talks on Clean Air Anger Environmental Groups." *Congressional Quarterly Weekly Report,* pp. 386–87.

———. 3 March 1990. "Senate–White House Deal Breaks Clean-Air Logjam." *Congressional Quarterly Weekly Report,* pp. 652–54.

———. 26 May 1990. "Easy House Vote on Clean Air Bodes Well for Bill's Future." *Congressional Quarterly Weekly Report,* pp. 1643–45.

Hahn, Robert W., and Gordon L. Hester. 1989. "Where Did All the Markets Go? An Analysis of EPA's Emissions Trading Program." *Yale Journal on Regulation* 6: 109–53.

Hartzog, George B., Jr. 1988. *Battling for the National Parks*. Mount Kisco, N.Y.: Moyer Bell.

Harvey, Mark W.T. 1991. "Echo Park, Glen Canyon, and the Postwar Wilderness Movement." *Pacific Historical Review* 60 (February): 43–67.

Hays, Samuel P. 1959. *Conservation and the Gospel of Efficiency: The Progressive Conservation Movement, 1890–1920*. Cambridge, Mass.: Harvard University Press.

———. 1987. *Beauty, Health, and Permanence: Environmental Politics in the United States, 1955–1985*. Cambridge: Cambridge University Press.

———. 1997. "From Conservation to Environment: Environmental Politics in the United States since World War II." In *Out of the Woods*, ed. Char Miller and Hal Rothman. Pittsburgh, Pa.: Pittsburgh University Press.

———. 1998. *Explorations in Environmental History*. Pittsburgh, Pa.: University of Pittsburgh Press.

Hayward, Clarissa Rile. 1998. "De-Facing Power." *Polity* 31 (Fall): 1–22.

Heclo, Hugh. 1978. "Issue Networks and the Executive Establishment." In *The New American Political System*, ed. Anthony King. Washington, D.C.: American Enterprise Institute for Public Policy Research.

Heinz, John P., Edward O. Laumann, Robert L. Nelson, and Robert H. Salisbury. 1993. *The Hollow Core: Private Interests in National Policymaking*. Cambridge, Mass.: Harvard University Press.

Hidy, Ralph W., Frank E. Hill, and Allan Nevins. 1963. *Timber and Men: The Weyerhaeuser Story*. New York: Macmillan.

Hildebrand, Joel. 1974. Interview by Ann Lage and Ray Lage. San Francisco: Sierra Club History Committee.

Hirt, Paul W. 1994. *A Conspiracy of Optimism: Management of the National Forests since World War Two*. Lincoln: University of Nebraska Press.

Hook, Janet. 12 May 1990. "By Shifting Tactics on Clean Air, Dingell Guarded His Power." *Congressional Quarterly Weekly Review*, pp. 1453–54, 1456.

Hosmer, Ralph S. 1940. "The Society of American Foresters: An Historical Summary." *Journal of Forestry* 38: 837–54.

———. 1945. "Some Recollections of Gifford Pinchot, 1898–1904." *Journal of Forestry* 43: 558–62.

Ingram, Helen M., and Dean Mann. 1989. "Interest Groups and Environmental Policy." In *Environmental Politics and Policy: Theories and Evidence*, ed. James P. Lester. Durham, N.C.: Duke University Press.

Ise, John. 1961. *Our National Park Policy: A Critical History*. Baltimore: Johns Hopkins Press.

Janofsky, Michael. 25 July 1999. "National Parks, Strained by Record Crowds, Face a Crisis." *New York Times*, p. 1.

Jones, Charles O. 1975. *Clean Air*. Pittsburgh, Pa.: University of Pittsburgh Press.

Jones, Holway R. 1965. *John Muir and the Sierra Club: The Battle for Yosemite*. San Francisco: Sierra Club.

Joskow, Paul L., and Richard Schmalensee. 1998. "The Market for Sulfur Dioxide Emissions." *American Economic Review* 88 (September): 669–85.

Kaufman, Herbert. 1960. *The Forest Ranger*. Baltimore: Johns Hopkins University Press.

Klyza, Christopher McGrory. 1992. "A Window of Autonomy: State Autonomy and the Forest Service in the Early 1900s." *Polity* (Winter) 25: 173–96.

———. 1994. "Ideas, Institutions, and Policy Patterns: Hardrock Mining, Forestry, and Grazing Policy on United States Public Lands, 1870–1985." *Studies in American Political Development* 8 (Fall): 341–74.

———. 1996. *Who Controls the Public Lands? Mining, Forestry, and Grazing Policies, 1870–1990*. Chapel Hill: University of North Carolina Press.

Kolko, Gabriel. 1977. *The Triumph of Conservatism: A Reinterpretation of American History, 1900–1916*. New York: Free Press. (Originally published in 1963.)

Kraft, Michael E. 1994. "Environmental Gridlock: Searching for Consensus in Congress." In *Environmental Policy in the 1990s*, 2d ed., ed. N. J. Vig and M. E. Kraft. Washington, D.C.: Congressional Quarterly Press.

———. 1997. "Environmental Policy in Congress: Revolution, Reform, or Gridlock?" In *Environmental Policy in the 1990s*, 3d ed., ed. N. J. Vig and M. E. Kraft. Washington, D.C.: Congressional Quarterly Press.

Krasner, Stephen D. 1978. *Defending the National Interest: Raw Materials Investments and U.S. Foreign Policy*. Princeton, N.J.: Princeton University Press.

Kriz, Margaret E. 23 September 1989. "Trouble by the Gallon for Carmakers." *National Journal*, p. 2320.

———. 9 December 1989. "Ahead of the Feds." *National Journal*, pp. 2989–93.

———. 27 January 1990. "Turbulence Ahead for Clean Air Act?" *National Journal*, pp. 223–24.

———. 2 June 1990. "Politics at the Pump." *National Journal*, pp. 1328–32.

Kunioka, Todd, and Lawrence S. Rothenberg. 1993. "The Politics of Bureaucratic Competition: The Case of Natural Resource Policy." *Journal of Policy Analysis and Management* 12: 700–25.

Lamare, James W. 1994. *California Politics: Economic, Power, and Policy*. New York: West.

Lane, Franklin K. 13 May 1918. "To Director of the National Park Service, Stephen T. Mather." In *America's National Park System: The Critical Documents*, ed. Lary Dilsaver. Lanham, Md.: Rowman & Littlefield.

Laxton, Josephine. 1931. "Pioneers in Forestry at Biltmore." *American Forests* 37 (May): 269–72, 319.

Lindblom, Charles E. 1977. *Politics and Markets: The World's Political-Economic Systems*. New York: Basic Books.

———. 1983. "Comment on Manley." *American Political Science Review* 77 (June): 384–86.

Lippman, Thomas W. 12 June 1990. "Gasoline Formula Fuels Controversy." *Washington Post*, p. D1.

Lowi, Theodore J. 1979. *The End of Liberalism: The Second Republic of the United States*. New York: Norton.

Lowry, William R. 1992. *The Dimensions of Federalism: State Governments and Pollution Control Policies*. Durham, N.C.: Duke University Press.

———. 1994. *The Capacity for Wonder*. Washington, D.C.: Brookings Institute.

———. 1998. *Preserving Public Lands for the Future: The Politics of Intergenerational Goods*. Washington, D.C.: Georgetown University Press.

Luger, Stan. 2000. *Corporate Power, American Democracy, and the Automobile Industry*. Cambridge: Cambridge University Press.

"Lumberman and Lumber Journals." 1910. *American Forestry* 16 (June): 381.

Madison, Christopher. 7 October 1989. "Congressional Focus." *National Journal*, p. 2491.

Manley, John F. 1983. "Neo-Pluralism: A Class Analysis of Pluralism I and Pluralism II." *American Political Science Review* 77 (June): 368–83.

Marsh, George Perkins. 1965. *Man and Nature*. Edited by David Lowenthal. Cambridge: Belknap Press of Harvard. Original published in 1864.

Mather, Stephen T. 1915. "The National Parks on a Business Basis." *American Review of Reviews* 51 (April) : 429–31.

Matthews, Jay. 29 September 1989. "Stringent Smog Control Approved in California." *Washington Post*, p. A3.

McCloskey, Michael. 1966. "The Wilderness Act of 1964: Its Background and Meaning." *Oregon Law Review* 45: 288–321.

McConnell, Grant. 1966. *Private Power and American Democracy*. New York: Knopf.

McCool, Daniel. 1998. "Field Essay: The Subsystem Family of Concepts: A Critique and a Proposal." *Political Research Quarterly* 51 (June): 551–70.

McFarland, Andrew S. 1987. "Interest Groups and Theories of Power in America." *British Journal of Political Science* 17 (April): 129–47.

———. 1991. "Interest Groups and Political Time: Cycles in America." *British Journal of Political Science* 21 (July): 257–86.

———. 1992. "Interest Groups and the Policymaking Process: Sources of Countervailing Power in America." In *The Politics of Interests: Interest Groups Transformed*, ed. Mark P. Petracca. Boulder, Colo.: Westview Press.

McGeary, Nelson M. 1960. *Gifford Pinchot: Forester and Politician*. Princeton, N.J.: Princeton University Press.

McKay, Douglas. 2 September 1953. "To John D. Rockefeller, Jr." Sleepy Hollow, N.Y.: Rockefeller Archive Center.

McPhee, John. 1970. *Encounters with the Archdruid*. New York: Farrar, Straus, & Giroux.

Melnick, R. Shep. 1992. "Pollution Deadlines and the Coalition for Failure." In *Environmental Politics: Public Costs, Private Rewards*, ed. Michael S. Grave and Fred L. Smith, Jr. New York: Praeger.

Milbrath, Lester W. 1989. *Envisioning a Sustainable Society: Learning Our Way Out*. Albany: State University of New York Press.

Miliband, Ralph. 1969. *The State in Capitalist Society*. New York: Basic Books.

Mills, C. Wright. 1956. *The Power Elite*. New York: Oxford University Press.

Mintz, Beth. 1975. "The President's Cabinet, 1897–1972." *Insurgent Sociologist* 5: 131–48.

Mintz, Beth, and Michael Schwartz. 1985. *The Power Structure of American Business*. Chicago: University of Chicago Press.

Mintz, Joel A. 1995. *Enforcement at the EPA*. Austin: University of Texas Press.

Mitchell, Timothy. 1991. "The Limits of the State: Beyond Statist Approaches and Their Critics." *American Political Science Review* 85 (March): 77–96.

Monroe, James P. 2001. *The Political Party Matrix: The Persistence of Organization*. Albany: State University of New York Press.

Morrison, Ernest. 1995. *J. Horace McFarland: A Thorn for Beauty*. Harrisburg, Pa.: Pennsylvania Historical and Museum Commission.

Mowry, George E. 1951. *The California Progressives*. Berkeley: University of California Press.

Nash, Roderick. 1982. *Wilderness and the American Mind.* New Haven, Conn.: Yale University Press.

Nie, Norman H., Sidney Verba, and John R. Petrocik. 1979. *The Changing American Voter.* Cambridge, Mass.: Harvard University Press.

Nieves, Evelyn, and Matthew L. Wald. 28 March 2000. "Park Service Plan Would Restore Wilderness to Yosemite." *New York Times:* www.nytimes.com/library/nat . . . ce/032800sci-environ-yosemite.html.

Noble, David F. 1977. *America by Design.* New York: Knopf.

Nordlinger, Eric A. 1981. *On the Autonomy of the Democratic State.* Cambridge, Mass.: Harvard University Press.

O'Connor, James. 1973. *The Fiscal Crisis of the State.* New York: St. Martin's.

Olson, Mancur. 1971. *The Logic of Collective Action: Public Goods and the Theory of Groups.* Cambridge, Mass.: Harvard University Press.

Orsi, Richard J. 1985. " 'Wilderness Saint' and 'Robber Baron': The Anomalous Partnership of John Muir and the Southern Pacific Company for Preservation of Yosemite National Park." *Pacific Historian* 29 (Summer–Fall): 136–52.

O'Toole, Randal. 1988. *Reforming the Forest Service.* Washington, D.C.: Island.

Parsons, Michael D. 1999. "The Problem of Power." *Policy Studies Review* 16 (Fall–Winter): 278–310.

Patterson, Jerry E. 1989. *The Vanderbilts.* New York: Abrams.

Penick, James. 1968. *Progressive Politics and Conservation: The Ballinger–Pinchot Affair.* Chicago: University of Illinois Press.

"People." 14 April 1990. *National Journal,* p. 916.

"People: Air Forces." 21 April 1990. *National Journal,* p. 986.

Perez-Pena, Richard. 7 November 1999. "Pataki to Impose Strict New Limits on Auto Emissions." *New York Times,* p. A1.

Pincetl, Stephanie. 1999. *Transforming California: A Political History of Land Use and Development.* Baltimore: Johns Hopkins University Press.

Pinchot, Gifford, and Henry S. Graves. 1896. *The White Pine: A Study.* New York: Century.

Pinchot, Gifford. 1899. "The Profession of Forestry." *Forester* 5: 155–60.

———. 1987. *Breaking New Ground.* Washington, D.C.: Island. Original published in 1947.

Pinkett, Harold T. 1958. "Gifford Pinchot, Consulting Forester, 1893–1898." *New York History* 34 (January): 34–49.

———. 1970. *Gifford Pinchot: Private and Public Forester.* Chicago: University of Illinois Press.

Pisani, Donald J. 1996. *Water, Land, and Law in the West: The Limits of Public Policy, 1850–1920.* Lawrence: University Press of Kansas.

———. 1997. "Forests and Conservation, 1865–1890." In *American Forest: Nature, Culture, and Politics,* ed. Char Miller. Lawrence: University Press of Kansas.

Piven, Frances, and Richard Cloward. 1982. *The New Class War: Reagan's Attack on the Welfare State and Its Consequences.* New York: Pantheon.

Polsby, Nelson. 1983. *Consequences of Party Reform.* New York: Oxford University Press.

Ponder, Stephen. 1987. "Gifford Pinchot: Press Agent for Forestry." *Journal of Forest History* 31 (January): 26–35.

Poulantzas, Nicos. 1973. *Political Power and Social Classes.* London: New Left Books.

Price, Overton W. 1914. "George W. Vanderbilt, Pioneer in Forestry." *American Forestry* 20: 420–25.

Pytte, Alyson. 27 October 1990. "A Decade's Acrimony Lifted in the Glow of Clean Air." *Congressional Quarterly Weekly Report*, pp. 3587–92.

Rhodes, R. A. W. 1988. *Beyond Westminster and Whitehall.* London: Unwin & Hyman.

Richardson, Elmo R. 1962. *The Politics of Conservation: Crusades and Controversies 1897–1913.* Berkeley: University of California Press.

Ridge, John Hiski. 1994. "Deconstructing the Clean Air Act: Examining the Controversy Surrounding Massachusetts's Adoption of the California Low Emission Vehicle Program." *Boston College Environmental Affairs Law Review* 22 (Fall): 163–99.

Righter, Robert W. 1982. *Crucible for Conservation: The Struggle for Grand Teton National Park.* Boulder: Colorado Associated University Press.

Robbins, William. 1982. *Lumberjacks and Legislators: Political Economy of the U.S. Lumber Industry, 1890–1941.* College Station: Texas A&M University Press.

———. 1997. "The Social Context of Forestry: The Pacific Northwest in the Twentieth Century." In *American Forest: Nature, Culture, and Politics,* ed. Char Miller. Lawrence: University Press of Kansas.

Rockefeller, John D., Jr. 15 August 1924. "To Horace M. Albright." Sleepy Hollow, N.Y.: Rockefeller Archive Center.

———. 19 July 1939. "To Horace M. Albright." Sleepy Hollow, N.Y.: Rockefeller Archive Center.

———. 27 November 1942. "To the Secretary of the Interior, Harold L. Ickes." Sleepy Hollow, N.Y.: Rockefeller Archive Center.

———. 5 January 1943. "To the Secretary of the Interior, Harold L. Ickes." Sleepy Hollow, N.Y.: Rockefeller Archive Center.

———. 10 February 1943. "To the President of the United States, Franklin Roosevelt." Sleepy Hollow, N.Y.: Rockefeller Archive Center.

———. 21 August 1953. "To Nelson A. Rockefeller." Sleepy Hollow, N.Y.: Rockefeller Archive Center.

———. 5 September 1953. "To the Secretary of the Interior, Douglas McKay." Sleepy Hollow, N.Y.: Rockefeller Archive Center.

———. 10 December 1953. "To President Dwight Eisenhower." Sleepy Hollow, N.Y.: Rockefeller Archive Center.

Rodgers, Andrew D., III. 1991. *Bernhard Edward Fernow: A Story of North American Forestry.* Princeton, N.J.: Princeton University Press.

Roper, Laura Wood. 1983. *FLO: A Biography of Frederick Law Olmsted.* Baltimore: Johns Hopkins University Press.

Rose, Fred. 2000. *Coalitions across the Class Divide: Lessons from the Labor, Peace, and Environmental Movements.* Ithaca, N.Y.: Cornell University Press.

Rosenbaum, Walter A. 1998. *Environmental Politics and Policy.* 4th ed. Washington, D.C.: Congressional Quarterly Press.

Rothman, Hal. 1998. *Devil's Bargains: Tourism in the Twentieth-Century American West.* Lawrence: University Press of Kansas.

———. 1999. "Tourism as Colonial Economy: Power and Place in Western Tourism." In *Power and Place in the North American West,* ed. Richard White and John M. Findlay. Seattle: University of Washington Press.

Roy, William. 1997. *Socializing Capital: The Rise of the Large Industrial Corporation in America*. Princeton, N.J.: Princeton University Press.

Runte, Alfred. 1973. " 'Worthless' Lands—Our National Parks." *American West* 10 (May): 4–11.

———. 1974. "Pragmatic Alliance: Western Railroads and the National Parks." *National Parks & Conservation Magazine* 48 (April): 14–21.

———. 1997. *National Parks: The American Experience*. 3d ed. Lincoln: University of Nebraska Press.

Sabatier, Paul A., ed. 1999. *Theoretical Lenses on Public Policy*. Boulder, Colo.: Westview.

Schnattschneider, E. E. 1960. *The Semisovereign People*. New York: Holt, Rinehart & Winston.

Schlozman, Kay L., and John T. Tierney. 1986. *Organized Interests and American Democracy*. New York: Harper & Row.

Schneider, Keith. 9 October 1990. "As Session Nears End, Revisers of the Clean Air Act Deadlock Over a New Proposal." *New York Times*, p. A18.

———. 23 October 1990. "Lawmakers Reach an Accord on Reductions of Air Pollution." *New York Times*, p. A1.

———. 28 October 1990. "How Clean Air Became Part of the Bottom Line." *New York Times*, sect. 4, p. 4.

Schrepfer, Susan R. 1983. *The Fight to Save the Redwoods: A History of Environmental Reform, 1917–1978*. Madison: University of Wisconsin Press.

Sellars, Richard West. 1997. *Preserving Nature in the National Parks: A History*. New Haven, Conn.: Yale University Press.

Sellers, Christopher. 1999. "Body, Place and the State: The Makings of an 'Environmentalist' Imaginary in the Post–World War II U.S." *Radical History Review* 74 (Spring): 31–64.

Shabecoff, Philip. 1 March 1989. "Health Risk from Smog Is Growing, Official Says." *New York Times*, p. A16.

———. 11 March 1989. "New Curbs on Gasoline by EPA." *New York Times*, sect. 1, p. 35.

———. 23 March 1989. "U.S. Calls Poisoning of Air Far Worse Than Expected and Threat to Public." *New York Times*, p. B11.

———. 13 April 1989. "Industrial Pollution Called Startling." *New York Times*, p. D21.

———. 2 March 1990. "Senators Achieve Accord with Bush on Clean Air Bill." *New York Times*, p. A1.

Shaiko, Ronald. 1999. *Voices and Echoes for the Environment*. New York: Columbia University Press.

Shankland, Robert. 1970. *Steve Mather of the National Parks*. New York: Knopf.

Sherman, E. A. 1926. "Thirty-Five Years of National Forest Growth." *Journal of Forestry* 24: 129–35.

Skocpol, Theda. 1979. *States and Social Revolutions*. Cambridge: Cambridge University Press.

———. 1980. "Political Response to Capitalist Crisis: Neo-Marxist Theories of the State and the Case of the New Deal." *Politics and Society* 10: 155–201.

———. 1985. "Bringing the State Back In: Strategies of Analysis in Current Research." In *Bringing the State Back In*, ed. Peter Evans, Dietrich Rueschemeyer, and Theda Skocpol. Cambridge: Cambridge University Press.

————. 1986/87. "A Brief Response [to G. William Domhoff]." *Politics and Society* 15: 331–32.

————. 1992. *Protecting Soldiers and Mothers: The Political Origins of Social Policy in the United States*. Cambridge, Mass.: Harvard University Press.

Skocpol, Theda, and Kenneth Finegold. 1982. "State Capacity and Economic Intervention in the Early New Deal." *Political Science Quarterly* 97 (Summer): 258–78.

Skocpol, Theda, and John Ikenberry. 1983. "The Political Formation of the American Welfare State in Historical and Comparative Perspective." *Comparative Social Research* 6: 87–148.

Skocpol, Theda, Marshall Ganz, and Ziad Munson. 2000. "A Nation of Organizers: The Institutional Origins of Civic Voluntarism in the United States." *American Political Science Review* 94 (September): 527–46.

Skowronek, Stephen. 1982. *Building a New American State: The Expansion of National Administrative Capacities, 1877–1920*. Cambridge: Cambridge University Press.

Smith, Herbert A. 1938. "The Early Forestry Movement in the United States." *Agricultural History* 12: 326–46.

Smith, Zachary A. 2000. *The Environmental Policy Paradox*. Englewood Cliffs, N.J.: Simon & Schuster.

Snow, Donald. 1992. *Inside the Environmental Movement: Meeting the Leadership Challenge*. Washington, D.C.: Island.

Steen, Harold. 1997. "The Beginning of the National Forest System." In *American Forest: Nature, Culture, and Politics*, ed. Char Miller. Lawrence: University Press of Kansas.

Stevenson, Richard W. 27 September 1990. "California to Get Tougher Air Rules." *New York Times*, p. A1.

Swain, Donald C. 1970. *Wilderness Defender: Horace M. Albright and Conservation*. Chicago: University of Chicago Press.

Tarrow, Sidney. 1994. *Power in Movement: Social Movements, Collective Action, and Politics*. New York: Cambridge University Press.

Taylor, Bob Pepperman. 1992. *Our Limits Transgressed: Environmental Political Thought in America*. Lawrence: University of Kansas Press.

Truman, David B. 1951. *The Governmental Process: Political Interests and Public Opinion*. New York: Knopf.

Twight, Ben W., and Fremont J. Lyden. 1989. "Measuring Forest Service Bias." *Journal of Forestry* 87 (May): 35–41.

Twight, Ben W., Fremont J. Lyden, and E. Thomas Tuchmann. 1990. "Constituency Bias in a Federal Career System? A Study of District Rangers of the U.S. Forest Service." *Administration and Society* 22 (November): 358–59.

U.S. Congress. 1990a. *Alternative Fuels: Hearing Before the Subcommittee on Environmental Protection of the Committee on Environment and Public Works, U.S. Senate, January 11, 1990, No. 101–584*. Washington D.C.: Government Printing Office.

————. 1990b. *Hearings before the Subcommittee on Energy and Power of the Committee on Energy and Commerce. U.S. House of Representatives, Oct 18–19 1989, No. 101–120*. Washington D.C.: Government Printing Office.

U.S. Department of Agriculture. 1904. *Annual Reports of the Department of Agriculture: 1904*. Washington, D.C.: Government Printing Office.

———. 1909. *Annual Reports of the Department of Agriculture: 1908.* Washington, D.C.: Government Printing Office.

U.S. Department of the Interior. 1912. "Proceedings of the National Park Conference: Held at the Yellowstone National Park, September 11 and 12, 1911." Washington, D.C.: Government Printing Office.

U.S. Environmental Protection Agency. 1990. *Toxics in the Community, 1988: National and Local Perspectives.* Washington, D.C.: Government Printing Office.

———. 1995. *National Air Pollutant Emissions Trends, 1990–1994.* Research Triangle Park, N.C.: Office of Air Quality Planning and Standards.

———. 1996. *1994 Toxics Release Inventory.* Washington, D.C.: Office of Pollution and Toxics.

U.S. General Accounting Office. 1995. *Forest Service: Distribution of Timber Sales Receipts, Fiscal Years 1992–94.* Washington, D.C.: U.S. General Accounting Office.

———. 1998. *Forest Service: Distribution of Timber Sales Receipts, Fiscal Years 1995–1997.* Washington, D.C.: Government Printing Office.

Useem, Michael. 1984. *The Inner Circle: Large Corporations and the Rise of Business Political Activity in the U.S. and U.K.* Oxford: Oxford University Press.

Vogel, David. 1989. *Fluctuating Fortunes.* New York: Basic Books.

Vos, Robert O. 1997. "Competing Approaches to Sustainability: Dimensions of Controversy." In *Flashpoints in Environmental Policymaking: Controversies in Achieving Sustainability,* ed. Sheldon Kamieniecki, George A. Gonzalez, and Robert O. Vos. Albany: State University of New York Press.

Wald, Matthew L. 6 March 1989. "States' Rules on Gasoline Are Resisted." *New York Times,* p. D1.

———. 25 March 1989. "EPA Backing States on Gasoline Vapor." *New York Times,* sect. 1, p. 35.

———. 7 April 1989. "Alternative-Fuel Vehicles Move from Fancy to Fact." *New York Times,* p. A1.

———. 11 August 1989. "Northeastern States Move to Restrict Pollution by Cars." *New York Times,* p. A1.

———. 10 October 1989. "Recharting War on Smog." *New York Times,* p. A1.

———. 25 September 1990. "White House Objects to Bills on Cleaner Fuel." *New York Times,* p. A24.

Walker, Jack L. 1983. "The Origins and Maintenance of Interest Groups in America." *American Political Science Review* 77 (June): 390–406.

———. 1991. *Mobilizing Interest Groups in America.* Ann Arbor: University of Michigan Press.

Ware, Alan. 1996. *Political Parties and Party Systems.* New York: Oxford University Press.

Wattenberg, Martin. 1991. *The Rise of Candidate-Centered Politics: Presidential Elections of the 1980s.* Cambridge, Mass.: Harvard University Press.

Weber, Edward P. 1998. *Pluralism by the Rules: Conflict and Cooperation in Environmental Regulation.* Washington, D.C.: Georgetown University Press.

Weinstein, James. 1968. *The Corporate Ideal in the Liberal State: 1900–1918.* Boston: Beacon.

Weisskopf, Michael. 7 June 1989. "A Changed Equation on Pollution." *Washington Post,* p. A1.

———. 30 July 1989. "Behind Clean-Air Bill: A Balancing of Interests." *Washington Post*, p. A16.
———. 21 September 1989. "Auto Industry Rebuffed on Emissions." *Washington Post*, p. A4.
———. 10 October 1989. "Key Provision of Bush Clean-Air Bill under Siege." *Washington Post*, p. A4.
———. 12 October 1989. "House Panel Votes to Weaken Clean-Air Bill." *Washington Post*, p. A1.
———. 7 February 1990. "Tentative Agreement on Clean Air Criticized." *Washington Post*, p. A6.
———. 1 March 1990. "Senate, White House Negotiators Compromise on Auto Pollution Controls." *Washington Post*, p. A5.
———. 2 March 1990. "Clean Air Pact Ends Acid Rain Impasse." *Washington Post*, p. A1.
———. 19 April 1990. "From Fringe to Political Mainstream: Environmentalists Set Policy Agenda." *Washington Post*, p. A1.
———. 22 October 1990. "Conferees Reach Acid Rain Accord." *Washington Post*, p. A1.
———. 28 October 1990. "Clean Air 'Milestone' is Sent to President." *Washington Post*, p. A1.
West, Darrell, and Burdett A. Loomis. 1999. *The Sound of Money: How Political Interests Get What They Want.* New York: Norton.
White, Richard. 1991. *"It's Your Misfortune and None of My Own": A History of the American West.* Norman: University of Oklahoma Press.
Wilkinson, Charles F. 1992. *Crossing the Next Meridian: Land, Water, and the Future of the West.* Washington, D.C.: Island.
Wilson, James Q. 1980. "The Politics of Regulation." In *The Politics of Regulation*, ed. James Q. Wilson. New York: Basic Books.
Winks, Robin W. 1997. *Laurence S. Rockefeller: Catalyst for Conservation.* Washington, D.C.: Island.
Wirth, Conrad L. 1980. *Parks, Politics, and the People.* Norman: University of Oklahoma Press.
Worsnop, Richard L. 1993. "National Parks." *CQ Researcher* 3 (28 May): 457–80.
Yeager, Peter C. 1991. *The Limits of Law: The Public Regulation of Private Pollution.* Cambridge: Cambridge University Press.
Young, Terence. 1996. "Social Reform through Parks: The American Civic Association's Program for a Better America." *Journal of Historical Geography* 22: 460–72.

Index

Acadia National Park, 59n8, 65
Acker, W. B., 47
Advisory Board on National Parks, Historic Sites, Buildings, and Monuments, 53, 68
Albright, Horace, 50, 59n7, 76n2, 76n5, 90, 120; as director of National Park Service, 55, 56; and Jackson Hole, 71–76; post-National Park Service career, 66–69; relationship with John D. Rockefeller, Jr., 58n3, 65–66
American Bison Society, 80
American Civic Association, 47, 48, 57. *See also* American Planning and Civic Association
American Conservation Association, 69
American Economic Association, 25
American Forest Congress (1905), 33, 36, 37, 38, 40
American Forestry Association, 15, 25, 26, 28, 30, 37, 42n2, 82
American Game Association, 67
American Lung Association, 103
American Mining Congress, 37
American National Livestock Association, 37
American Petroleum Institute, 99, 100, 101

American Pioneer Trails Association, 67
American Planning and Civic Association, 67. *See also* American Civic Association
American Youth Hostel, 69
Appleton, Albert F., 108
Arcata Redwood Company, 89, 91, 93
Armes, William, 63
Army Corps of Engineers, 46
Atchison, Topeka & Sante Fe Railway System, 46
Ayres, Richard, 103, 106, 107, 109

Baker, John, 74
Baltimore and Ohio Railroad, 38
Becker, Bill, 110
Biltmore Estate, North Carolina, 25–26
Bliss, Cornelius, 29
Bohemian Club, 81, 87
Boone and Crockett Club, 67, 74, 80
Brandis, Sir Dietrich, 25, 29
Brookings Institute, 12
Brower, David, 83–87
Bryce Canyon, 47
Bryan, William Jennings, 41
Buckley, William P., 97
Buist, Donald R., 106

139

About the Author

George A. Gonzalez received his Ph.D. in 1997 from the University of Southern California and is currently an assistant professor in the Department of Political Science, University of Miami, Coral Gables, Florida. He is coeditor of *Flashpoints in Environmental Policymaking: Controversies in Achieving Sustainability*, which won the 1998 Lynton K. Caldwell book award, given by the Science, Technology, and Environmental Policy section of the American Political Science Association.